Pocket PC Database Development with Embedded Visual Basic

ROB TIFFANY

Apress™

Pocket PC Database Development with Embedded Visual Basic
Copyright ©2001 by Rob Tiffany

ISBN (pbk): 1-893115-65-8

Printed and bound in the United States of America 12345678910

Editorial Directors: Dan Appleman, Gary Cornell, Jason Gilmore, Karen Watterson
Technical Editor: James Beidleman
Managing Editor: Grace Wong
Marketing Manager: Stephanie Rodriguez
Copy Editor: Nicole LeClerc
Production Editor: Sofia Marchant
Compositor and Artist: Impressions Book and Journal Services, Inc.
Indexer: Nancy Guenther
Cover Designer: Karl Miyajima

Distributed to the book trade in the United States by Springer-Verlag New York, Inc., 175 Fifth Avenue, New York, NY, 10010
and outside the United States by Springer-Verlag GmbH & Co. KG, Tiergartenstr. 17, 69112 Heidelberg, Germany

In the United States, phone 1-800-SPRINGER; orders@springer-ny.com;
http://www.springer-ny.com
Outside the United States, contact orders@springer.de; http://www.springer.de;
fax +49 6221 345229

For information on translations, please contact Apress directly at 901 Grayson Street, Suite 204, Berkeley, CA, 94710
Phone: 510-549-5938; Fax: 510-549-5939; info@apress.com;
http://www.apress.com

The source code for this book is available to readers at http://www.apress.com. You will need to answer questions pertaining to this book in order to successfully download the code.

To my wife, Cathy.

Brief Contents

Contents

Chapter 7 Pocket Access Database Manager

Foreword

THERE HASN'T BEEN A better time to begin developing applications for handhelds. In the last four years, we have seen a tremendous leap in the functional capabilities offered by handheld computing platforms, which has culminated in the rich interfaces we see in the current crop of Windows CE–embedded systems.

The Pocket PC platform is particularly compelling because it is truly portable, and it has a great color interface and solid application integration with its desktop counterparts. In addition, most of these devices have sufficient processing power to incorporate advanced handheld appliance technologies—GPS, cellular communications, and so on. These advantages coupled with the new eMbedded Visual Tools suite from Microsoft make the Pocket PC a solid choice for mobile systems development in the next few years.

Whether these Windows CE devices are used to extend the reach of enterprise applications or as stand-alone information-gathering devices, eMbedded Visual Basic will be the logical choice for the legions of Visual Basic developers seeking to add mobile development expertise to their skill sets. At the heart of eMbedded Visual Basic's appeal is its support for ActiveX Data Objects for Windows CE (ADOCE). The combination of eMbedded Visual Basic and ADOCE significantly reduces the learning curve by enabling developers to manipulate databases objects in a manner similar to the desktop version of ADO.

If you've been waiting for the right time to start your handheld development career, wait no longer! Armed with a Pocket PC, eMbedded Visual Basic, this book, and a small measure of enthusiasm, you will produce handheld applications in very short order.

Sincerely,
Derek Mitchell
Chief Executive Officer
deVBuzz.com, Inc.

CHAPTER 1

Getting Started

IT'S VERY LIKELY THAT you picked up this book because you've never seen SQL, database development, the Pocket PC, and eMbedded Visual Basic 3.0 all put together in a book title before. We've now entered a new phase of computing that's dominated by small, handheld devices designed to make your life easier. These devices started out as nothing more than convenient, digital personal information managers. Thanks to the Microsoft Windows CE 3.0 operating system and the Pocket PC hardware platform, we now have a powerful force to be reckoned with in the client enterprise computing space. Powerful devices with increased RAM, fast RISC processors, wireless capabilities, and built-in networking are only half of the good news. The other half is that your old friends Visual Basic, COM, Access, and ADO have all come along for the ride. The aim of this book is to help you take the new, miniaturized, versions of these old desktop friends and make you a productive developer of database applications on the Pocket PC. In order to do that, I'll have to illustrate the capabilities and limitations of these new embedded tools and technologies.

Who This Book Is For

This book targets the millions of Visual Basic 6.0 database programmers who are ready to make the jump to the Pocket PC. Furthermore, this book assumes that you have experience working with ActiveX Data Objects (ADO) to communicate with desktop databases, such as Microsoft Access, and remote server databases, such as Microsoft SQL Server. With this kind of experience, you should have no trouble working with eMbedded Microsoft technologies such as Pocket Access, ADOCE, and eMbedded Visual Basic 3.0.

Installing and Configuring Your Development Environment

The first thing I'll discuss is the proper installation and configuration of the software required to begin developing for the Pocket PC. You're probably thinking that a book focused on SQL database development for the Pocket PC shouldn't waste space teaching developers how to set up their computers. Trust me, I won't do this on my next Pocket PC development book. The reality is, I've personally

1

experienced so much quirkiness in working with these tools on the various supported platforms that I can't guarantee that you'll be successful unless I hold your hand and walk you through the process. I can't make the assumption that everyone is feeling right at home with a new operating system, new hardware, and new tools.

The Structured Query Language

Once you have a working development environment, I'll move on to the subset of the Structured Query Language (SQL) that you'll be allowed to use in your Pocket PC database development. I'll cover the applicable SQL Data Definition Language (DDL) that enables you to create and manipulate databases, tables, and indexes. I'll follow that up by covering the applicable SQL Data Manipulation Language (DML) that enables you to insert, retrieve, and delete data in your database.

NOTE *From now on, I'll refer to the subset of SQL that we're allowed to use on the Pocket PC as Pocket SQL.*

Using ADOCE

Armed with an understanding of Pocket SQL, we'll explore the world of the Microsoft ActiveX Data Objects for Windows CE (ADOCE). ADOCE is a subset of the desktop and server versions of ADO and it enables you to work with local Pocket Access databases as well as remote SQL Server databases. Using both the ADOCE Connection object and Recordset object, I'll show you how to connect to data sources, interact with data, perform transactions, and deal with errors.

NOTE *The terms "Pocket Access" and "Windows CE databases" are often used synonymously. Used in this context, Pocket Access shouldn't be confused with the graphical version of Access that runs on the Handheld PC.*

Importing and Exporting Data with ActiveSync

Not only does ActiveSync act as the primary conduit between the Pocket PC and your desktop computer, it also provides several features that allow for the manual import and export of databases, tables, and data between the two. On the desktop/server side of things, ActiveSync can work with Access databases or any ODBC data source. On the handheld side of things, ActiveSync works with Pocket Access databases. ActiveSync gives you a powerful tool to keep databases on your handheld synched up with databases on your desktop or on a server.

Building Database Applications

Taking everything you've learned about Pocket SQL and ADOCE, you'll put that knowledge to work to build a couple of database applications. Constructing a Pocket Access database manager serves not only to exploit all the functionality provided by ADOCE and Pocket SQL, but it's also a useful program to have when you need to build future Pocket Access databases. On the remote side of things, you'll build a full-featured eMbedded Visual Basic client to a SQL Server 2000 database that uses ActiveSync.

Installing the Tools

In order to get your development environment ready for Pocket PC programming, you must properly install and configure a number of software packages. The required software includes Microsoft ActiveSync 3.1 (it came with your Pocket PC), the Microsoft eMbedded Visual Tools 3.0, and the Pocket PC SDK.

ActiveSync Installation

Though you have numerous software tools and SDKs to install and configure, it's important to install Microsoft ActiveSync first because everything else relies on its existence. Additionally, I've experienced difficulties in the past getting the eMbedded Visual Tools to talk to the Pocket PC when ActiveSync was installed last. Therefore, I'm going to walk you through the ActiveSync Setup Wizard to ensure that you get it installed properly. ActiveSync is designed to run on Windows 98, Windows ME, Windows NT, and Windows 2000. Keep in mind that you will be unable to use your Pocket PC's USB cable if you're running Windows NT. When you pop in the ActiveSync CD, the initial setup dialog box should appear as shown in Figure 1-1. Go ahead and click Next to get started with the installation.

Figure 1-1. The first dialog box of the ActiveSync 3.1 Setup Wizard

Once ActiveSync is installed, it's time to get your device connected. Plug the USB cable that came with your Pocket PC into your computer's USB port and also ensure that it's connected to your Pocket PC. You should hear a musical chime from both your Pocket PC and your desktop computer when the two connect. Once the connection is made, you are prompted to create a new partnership, as shown in Figure 1-2. Go ahead and select Yes.

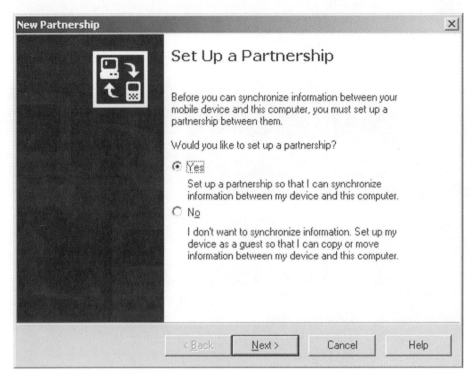

Figure 1-2. Creating a partnership in the ActiveSync Setup Wizard

At this point you'll have to decide if you want to create a partnership with just one or two computers. If you don't have a partnership in place with another computer, and you only wish to ActiveSync with a single PC, select Yes. If you have an existing partnership or you want to use a second computer, select No. Once you've decided on the number of partnerships you want, you'll need to decide which programs you want to synchronize with between your Pocket PC to your desktop computer, as shown in Figure 1-3. While you may or may not want to keep your Pocket PC synchronized with various Outlook components, you'll need to check Pocket Access, as you'll use that feature later in the book.

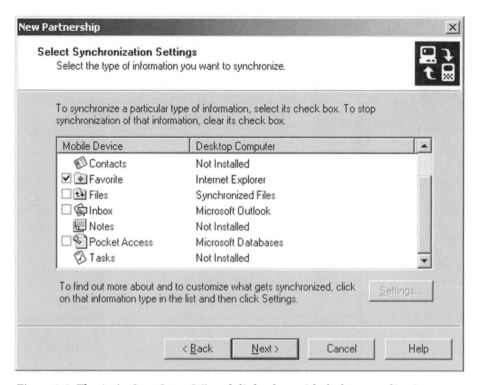

Figure 1-3. The ActiveSync Setup Wizard dialog box with desktop applications selected for synchronization

With your synchronization settings decided upon, the creation of your ActiveSync partnership is now complete and the ActiveSync setup is finished. As illustrated in Figure 1-4, the ActiveSync software now serves as the primary conduit between your Pocket PC and your desktop computer. In addition to USB, the ActiveSync software can also communicate with your Pocket PC through serial cable, infrared, and Ethernet. In the event that you have a few extra bucks left after buying your Pocket PC, get an Ethernet card for the fastest possible ActiveSync speed. If you take some time to get familiar with ActiveSync, you'll notice that it provides you with the following features:

- A file explorer that enables you to drag and drop files between your desktop computer and your Pocket PC

- A file backup and restore program to keep your Pocket PC data safe

- The ability to add and remove Pocket PC programs in the same manner as Windows on the desktop

- The previously mentioned ability to import and export databases and tables

- The ability to synchronize with various desktop and Internet applications

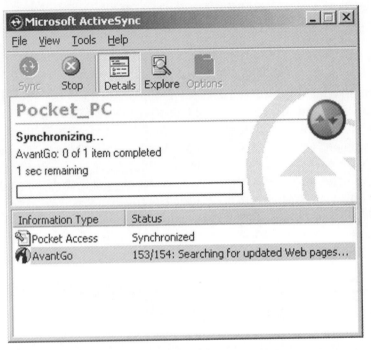

Figure 1-4. The ActiveSync software in the process of synchronizing offline Web pages

TIP *If you ever need to remove ActiveSync from your computer, navigate from the Windows Start button to Settings ➤ Control Panel. From there, double-click the Add/Remove Programs icon, select Microsoft ActiveSync 3.1, and then click the Change/Remove button to uninstall the program.*

eMbedded Visual Tools Installation

With ActiveSync now providing a pipeline between your desktop computer and your Pocket PC, it's time to install the eMbedded Visual Tools. Included in this installation are eMbedded Visual Basic, eMbedded Visual C++, various Platform SDKs, emulators, and online help. Your choice of desktop operating system plays a big role when it comes to developing Pocket PC software. If you're running Windows 98 or Windows ME, you can run and debug your eMbedded Visual Basic applications directly on your Pocket PC through USB, but you can't run or debug them in the Pocket PC emulator. If you're running Windows NT 4.0, you can run and debug your eMbedded Visual Basic applications in the Pocket PC emulator, but you'll be unable to do the same with USB on your handheld because Windows NT doesn't support USB. Windows 2000 is the preferred operating system for developing Pocket PC applications because it supports both the emulator and USB. I will use Windows 2000 as my platform in all the examples that I present throughout the book. Armed with the knowledge of what each desktop operating system buys you, let's move on to the installation. When you insert the Microsoft eMbedded Visual Tools 3.0 CD in your computer, the initial Setup Wizard dialog box displays on your screen, as shown in Figure 1-5. Click the Next button to get started with the installation.

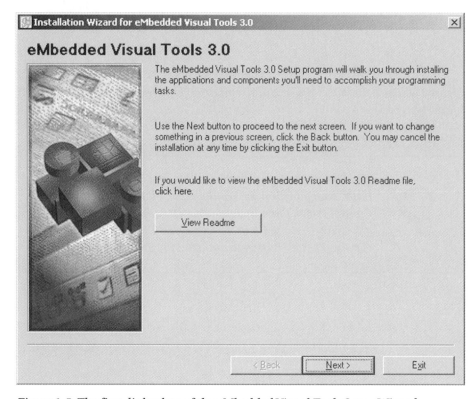

Figure 1-5. The first dialog box of the eMbedded Visual Tools Setup Wizard

When you get to the screen shown in Figure 1-6, make sure that you've checked both the eMbedded Visual Tools 3.0 and Microsoft Windows Platform SDK for Pocket PC options. You can also choose to install the SDKs for the Handheld PC and the Palm-size PC, but I don't cover those devices in this book.

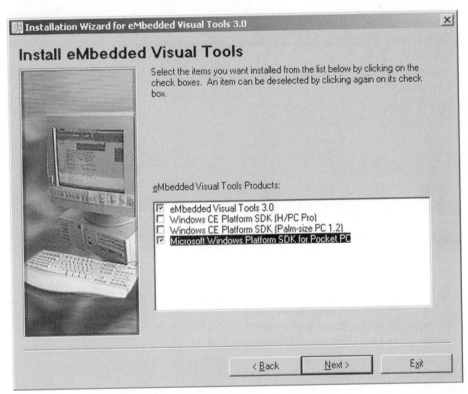

Figure 1-6. The eMbedded Visual Tools Setup Wizard dialog box where eMbedded Visual Tools and Platform SDKs are selected for installation

When you get to the screen shown in Figure 1-7, make sure you check both the eMbedded Visual Basic 3.0 and Common Components options. You may optionally install eMbedded Visual C++ 3.0, but I don't cover that language in this book.

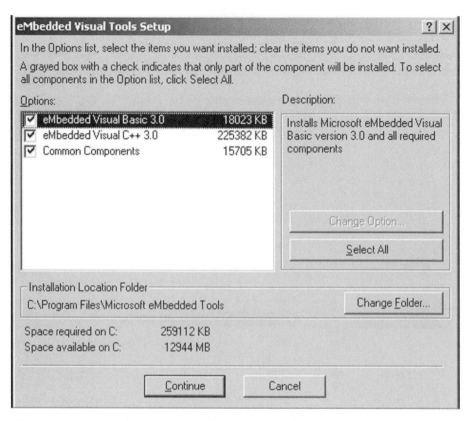

Figure 1-7. The eMbedded Visual Tools Setup Wizard dialog box with languages and components selected

 TIP *If you ever need to remove the eMbedded Visual Tools from your computer, navigate from the Windows Start button to Settings ➤ Control Panel. From there, double-click the Add/Remove Programs icon, select Microsoft eMbedded Visual Tools, and then click the Change/Remove button to uninstall the program.*

Once the eMbedded Visual Tools are installed, the Setup Wizard moves on to install any of the Platform SDKs that you previously selected for installation. When you get to the screen shown in Figure 1-8, make sure you select Complete.

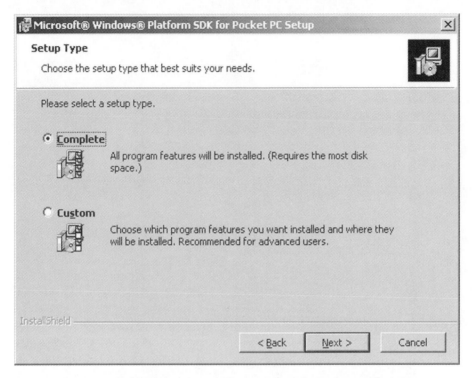

Figure 1-8. The eMbedded Visual Tools Setup Wizard dialog box with setup type selected

TIP *If you ever need to remove the Pocket PC SDK from your computer, navigate from the Windows Start button to Settings ➤ Control Panel. From there, double-click the Add/Remove Programs icon, select Microsoft Windows Platform SDK for Pocket PC, and then click the Change/Remove button to uninstall the program.*

Testing Your Installation

With ActiveSync, the eMbedded Visual Tools, and the Pocket PC SDK all installed on your desktop computer, it's time to test your installation. Start out by creating a Pocket PC project with eMbedded Visual Basic, as shown in Figure 1-9. You'll notice right away that eMbedded Visual Basic looks just like Visual Basic 6.0.

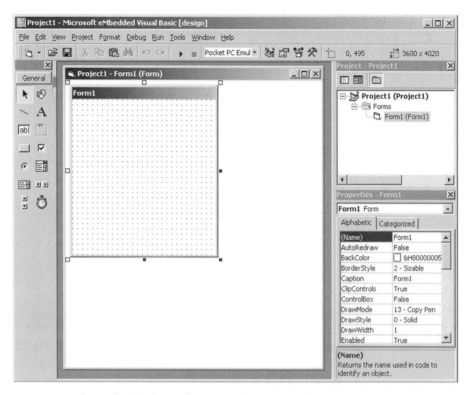

Figure 1-9. The eMbedded Visual Basic 3.0 integrated development environment

The eMbedded and desktop versions of Visual Basic look alike, both are easy to use, and both produce 32-bit applications, but the similarities end there. It would be accurate to characterize eMbedded Visual Basic as a language based on a version of VBScript that allows for the use of forms, modules, and ActiveX controls. Unfortunately, there are no class modules, you can't create COM DLLs, you can't build ActiveX controls, and everything's a Variant. Fortunately for us, eMbedded Visual Basic comes with ADOCE 3.0, so we can access both local and remote databases in a familiar way.

Connection Test

The next thing you need to test is eMbedded Visual Basic's capability to communicate with your Pocket PC through ActiveSync. In order to test this functionality, you'll need to go to the eMbedded Visual Basic menu and select Tools ➤ Remote Tools ➤ Configure Platform Manager to bring up the Windows CE Platform Manager Configuration screen shown in Figure 1-10.

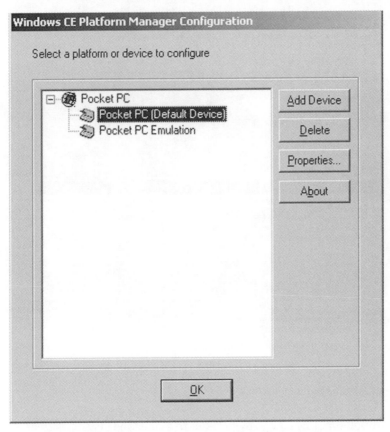

Figure 1-10. The Windows CE Platform Manager Configuration dialog box

Select the Pocket PC (Default Device) option and then click Properties to bring up the screen shown in Figure 1-11. With Microsoft ActiveSync selected, click Test to establish a connection to your device. The software will tell you when the connection has been made and a chime will sound. If your device isn't found and connected in ten seconds, it's time to go into troubleshooting mode.

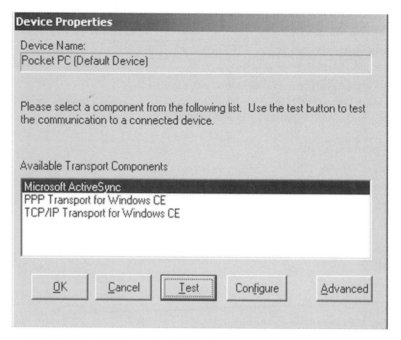

Figure 1-11. The Device Properties dialog box

Connection Troubleshooting

When troubleshooting connectivity between eMbedded Visual Basic and your
Pocket PC, eliminate all the obvious things first.

- Check to make sure your Pocket PC is fully charged or is plugged in.

- Check to make sure that your USB or serial cable is securely plugged into
  both your Pocket PC and your desktop computer.

- Ensure that your ActiveSync software shows your Pocket PC to be connected and that the circle on the right-hand side is green.

If all the items in the previous list check out, return to the screen shown in
Figure 1-11 to try out the remaining two transport components. Select TCP/IP
Transport for Windows CE and then click Test. You should see a file transfer dialog box indicating that the TCP/IP components are being copied to your Pocket
PC. Once the transfer is complete, the software will try to make a connection to
your Pocket PC. Like before, the software will notify you when the connection is
made and a musical chime will sound. If you're still not having any luck, select
PPP Transport for Windows CE and then click Test. As with the TCP/IP Transport,
you'll see the file copy progress of the relevant PPP components to your Pocket

PC. Hopefully, this time you'll achieve a connected state. If not, go back to your original selection of Microsoft ActiveSync and try the test again. I've heard of many cases when just the copying of the TCP/IP and PPP components to the Pocket PC made the ActiveSync Transport start working. If you're still dead in the water, remove and then reinstall the Pocket PC SDK. If all else fails, try a soft reset of your Pocket PC and then repeat all the previous troubleshooting measures.

> **NOTE** *For those of you who are new to the Pocket PC world, a soft reset is just like rebooting your computer. Because Pocket PCs don't have hard drives, all data and applications reside on a RAM disk. A soft reset enables you to reboot your Pocket PC without destroying your data. A hard reset, on the other hand, completely wipes away everything from memory and takes you back to the Pocket PC's original factory state. Be sure to consult the documentation that accompanies your Pocket PC to make sure that you push the right button when you want to reset your Pocket PC "softly."*

Emulator Test

Finally, to ensure that eMbedded Visual Basic and the emulator are talking to each other and functioning properly, build the obligatory "Hello World" application. From inside eMbedded Visual Basic, drag a CommandButton onto your main form. Double-click the CommandButton to bring up the code editor and insert the following line of code:

```
Msgbox "Hello World"
```

In the Devices combo box next to the Run icon on the toolbar, select Pocket PC Emulation. When you run this application in the emulator it should look like Figure 1-12. Make sure that when you click the CommandButton, a message box pops us that contains "Hello World!"

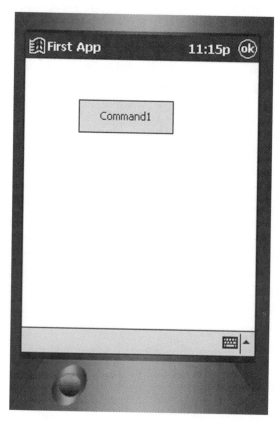

Figure 1-12. The Pocket PC emulator running the Hello World application

Device Test

Now go back to the Devices combo box on the toolbar and select Pocket PC (Default Device). This time when you run the application, you'll see a file transfer dialog box copying the required project files to your Pocket PC. When your Hello World application starts to run on your handheld, make sure everything is working properly. Assuming that everything worked as expected on your Pocket PC and in the emulator, it's time to leave behind installation and configuration and move on to learning Pocket SQL.

NOTE *Even though this chapter has included many references to the Pocket PC, getting it to communicate with your desktop computer, and running eMbedded Visual Basic applications on it, I don't want to alienate readers who don't actually own a Pocket PC. For those of you who own a computer running Windows NT or Windows 2000, you can download the eMbedded Visual Tools for free from the Microsoft Web site and realistically build almost any kind of Pocket PC application you want just using the emulator. In fact, that's exactly what I did! Therefore, one of the goals of this book will be to have as many examples as possible run in the emulator and not require an actual handheld device.*

CHAPTER 2

The Pocket SQL Data Definition Language

THE SQL DATA DEFINITION Language (DDL) specifies how various database objects are created, modified, and deleted. Normally these objects include such things as tables, views, privileges, indexes, triggers, and stored procedures. In Chapter 1, you learned that on the Pocket PC you're limited to using a subset of the Structured Query Language. It should then come as no surprise that you'll find yourself limited when it comes to the database objects you can work with. Those of you who are accustomed to using GUI tools, such as Microsoft Access or the SQL Server Enterprise Manager, to construct and modify databases are probably wondering why you even need to know the Pocket SQL DDL. The answer is simple: There is no GUI tool available to build and modify Pocket Access databases on the Pocket PC. Pocket Access databases have to be built programmatically using Pocket SQL DDL, eMbedded Visual Basic, and ADOCE. While it may seem like you're having to do things the hard way, you'll gain the skills you need to build your own Access-like GUI tool later on in this book.

 NOTE *As you work your way through this chapter, you'll notice consistent use of the ADOCE Recordset object in all the examples. The Pocket SQL DDL statements are executed using the Open method of the Recordset object. Even though I haven't covered the nuances of the ADOCE Recordset object yet, I think it's important to first learn the SQL syntax required to create, modify, and delete Pocket Access database objects. Chapter 5 discusses the Recordset object in great detail.*

Creating a Database

In order to create a Pocket Access database on your handheld, you must use the CREATE DATABASE statement. The specifics of creating a database, including the proper statement syntax, an explanation of parameters, the possible return values, and a working example, are as follows.

Syntax

CREATE DATABASE '*DatabaseName.cdb*'

Parameters

DatabaseName

This is the name of the database that's to be created. A valid path may be added in front of the database name. The optional path and required database name must be surrounded by single quotes and have the Pocket Access file extension (.cdb).

Return Values

None.

Example

In this example, you'll execute the CREATE DATABASE statement to create a TestDB.cdb database in the My Documents folder of the emulator. Before you get started with this code snippet, you must first set a reference to the Microsoft CE ADO Control 3.0 through the Project ➤ References menu. Additionally, you must add **3.0** after "Recordset" when you create your object to ensure that the proper version of ADOCE is referenced.

```
Dim RS As ADOCE.Recordset
Set RS = CreateObject("ADOCE.Recordset.3.0")
RS.Open "CREATE DATABASE '\My Documents\TestDB.cdb'"
Set RS = Nothing
```

Drawing upon your past ADO experience, you probably noticed a couple of things in the previous code snippet. First of all, you didn't have to use the ADOCE Connection object to connect to anything before executing your statement. Opening the Recordset with the statement and path to the new database are sufficient. The second thing that probably jumped out at you is that I didn't close the Recordset before dereferencing it. Without going into too much detail about ADOCE Recordset behavior, executing a DDL statement with the Open method doesn't leave you with an open Recordset. If you check the State of the Recordset just after executing your CREATE DATABASE statement, you'll see that it is closed.

TIP *If you are using a H/PC or CE 2.X, the previous CreateObject code should be changed to the following:*
`Set RS = CreateObject("ADOCE.Recordset")`
Everything else will work as stated.

Windows CE Remote File Viewer

At this point, you're probably wondering how to verify that the database you just created actually exists or not. Luckily, eMbedded Visual Basic provides you with a file explorer that not only enables you to see files on your Pocket PC, but also lets you view files inside the emulator. In order to activate the File Viewer, go to the eMbedded Visual Basic menu and select Tools ➤ Remote Tools ➤ File Viewer. With the File Viewer up and running, go to its menu and select Connection ➤ Add Connection to bring up the Select a Windows CE Device dialog box shown in Figure 2-1.

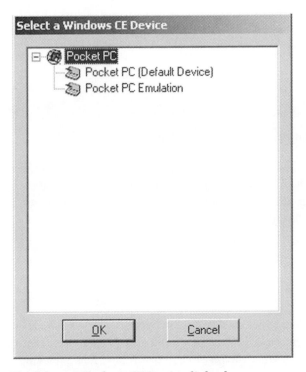

Figure 2-1. The Select a Windows CE Device dialog box

Highlight Pocket PC Emulation and click OK. The File Viewer then connects to the emulator's file system and displays a familiar directory tree. You're given the ability to import and export files between the device and the desktop. You can also create new folders and use the F5 key to refresh the display. Let's go find that database that you supposedly created by double-clicking the My Documents folder. Sure enough, TestDB.cdb should be sitting in the My Documents folder, as shown in Figure 2-2.

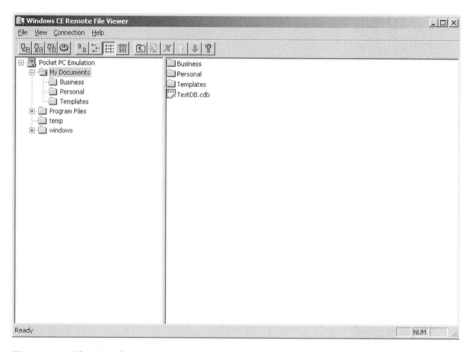

Figure 2-2. The Windows CE Remote File Viewer

NOTE *Creating a new database with the same name as an existing database in the same folder causes an application error.*

Deleting a Database

You can delete a Pocket Access database with the DROP DATABASE statement. The specifics of deleting a database, including the proper statement syntax, an explanation of parameters, the possible return values, and a working example, are as follows.

Syntax

DROP DATABASE '*DatabaseName.cdb*' [, *n*]

Parameters

DatabaseName

This is the name of the database that's to be deleted. A valid path may be added in front of the database name. The optional path and the required database name must be surrounded by single quotes and have the Pocket Access file extension (.cdb).

n

This represents any additional databases that are to be deleted in a comma-separated list.

Return Values

None.

Example

In this example, you'll execute the DROP DATABASE statement to delete the TestDB.cdb database that resides in the My Documents folder of the emulator.

```
Dim RS As ADOCE.Recordset
Set RS = CreateObject("ADOCE.Recordset.3.0")
RS.Open "DROP DATABASE '\My Documents\TestDB.cdb'"
Set RS = Nothing
```

Now that you've deleted the database in code, bring up the Windows CE Remote File Viewer to go see for yourself. If your File Viewer is already open, click F5 to refresh the display to confirm that TestDB.cdb no longer exists in the My Documents folder.

NOTE *Deleting a database that doesn't exist causes an application error.*

Creating a Table

Creating a table in an existing Pocket Access database requires the use of the CREATE TABLE statement. The specifics of creating a table, including the proper statement syntax, an explanation of parameters, the possible return values, and a working example, are as follows.

Syntax

CREATE TABLE *TableName* (*FieldName FieldType* [, *FieldName FieldType*])

Parameters

TableName

This is the name of the new table.

FieldName

This is the name of the column to create in the new table.

FieldType

This is the data type of the column. Valid data types are listed in Table 2-1.

Table 2-1. Valid Column Data Types

DATA TYPE	DESCRIPTION
Varchar[(n)]	This is a NULL-terminated Unicode character string of length *n*, with a maximum length of 255 characters. If *n* is not supplied, 1 is assumed.
Text	This is a variable-length string that can hold up to 32,000 characters.
Varbinary[(n)]	This is a binary value of less than 256. If *n* is not supplied, 1 is assumed.
Long Varbinary	This is a binary value of less then 65,469 bytes. This type is also known as OLE Object.
Int	This is a 4-byte signed integer.
Smallint	This is a 2-byte signed integer.
Float	This is a double-precision floating point value.
Datetime	This is a Data object value.
Bit	This is a Logical or Boolean value. Zero is FALSE and nonzero is TRUE.

Return Values

One of the following error values may be returned:

- E_OUTOFMEMORY

- DB_E_ERRORSINCOMMAND

- DB_E_DUPLICATETABLEID

- DB_E_DUPLICATECOLUMNID

Example

In this example, you'll execute the CREATE TABLE statement to create a new table called "Contacts" in the TestDB.cdb database that resides in the My Documents folder of the emulator. Unlike the previous examples, here you have to construct and execute a SQL statement that allows for the creation of the various fields in your Contacts table. Additionally, you have to execute this statement in the context of an implicit connection to the TestDB.cdb database. Without this implicit connection to indicate where the table belongs, the table would be created in the Pocket PC's internal system database, which I'll cover later on in the book.

```
Dim RS As ADOCE.Recordset
Dim SQL As String
Set RS = CreateObject("ADOCE.Recordset.3.0")
SQL = "CREATE TABLE Contacts ("
SQL = SQL & "ContactID int ,"
SQL = SQL & "FirstName varchar(30) ,"
SQL = SQL & "LastName varchar(30) ,"
SQL = SQL & "CompanyName varchar(50) ,"
SQL = SQL & "StreetAddress varchar(100) ,"
SQL = SQL & "City varchar(50) ,"
SQL = SQL & "State varchar(2) ,"
SQL = SQL & "Zip varchar(20) )"
RS.Open SQL, "\My Documents\TestDB.cdb"
Set RS = Nothing
```

If you want to see for yourself that the table and associated fields were all created, you'll need to open the newly created Contacts table and then loop through all the fields to display their names and data types.

```
Dim RS As ADOCE.Recordset
Dim i As Integer
Set RS = CreateObject("ADOCE.Recordset.3.0")
RS.Open "Contacts", "\My Documents\TestDB.cdb"
For i = 0 To RS.Fields.Count - 1
    MsgBox "Field Name: " & RS.Fields(i).Name & vbCrLf & _
        "Data Type: " & RS.Fields(i).Type
Next
RS.Close
Set RS = Nothing
```

Hopefully, upon running this code you had a message box pop up eight times displaying the proper field names in the proper order. You probably noticed that the data types are displayed as numbers that are meaningless to you. Those numbers correspond to the data type constants in Table 2-2.

Table 2-2. Data Type Constants

CONSTANT	NUMBER
adVarWChar	202
adLongVarWChar	203
adVarBinary	204
adLongVarBinary	205
adInteger	3
adSmallInt	2
adDouble	5
adDate	7
adBoolean	11

Armed with the information provided in Table 2-2, you can verify that the field data type numbers returned in the previous example are the same as the ones you used when you created the table.

 NOTE *Creating a table in a database where a table with the same name already exists causes an application error.*

Modifying a Table

In order to modify the structure of an existing table in a Pocket Access database, you must use the ALTER TABLE statement. The specifics of modifying a table, including the proper statement syntax, an explanation of parameters, the possible return values, and a working example, are as follows.

Syntax

ALTER TABLE *TableName* TO *TableName2*

ALTER TABLE *TableName* ADD *FieldName FieldType* [BEFORE *FieldName2*]

ALTER TABLE *TableName* DROP *FieldName*

ALTER TABLE *TableName* MOVE *FieldName* [BEFORE *FieldName2*]

ALTER TABLE *TableName* RENAME *FieldName* TO *FieldName2*

Parameters

TableName

This is the name of the table that you'll be making structural changes to.

TableName2

This is the name that an existing table will be changed to. A table with this same name cannot already exist in the database.

FieldName

This is the name of the column to add, remove, or rename. To add a column, a column with the same name cannot already exist in the table.

FieldName2

This is the name of another column in the table. In order to use the ADD and MOVE statements, the name must already exist in the table. The use of the RE-NAME statement requires that the name doesn't already exist.

FieldType

This is the data type for the column in question.

Return Values

None.

Examples

I'll explain the various uses of the ALTER TABLE statement through a series of five examples that illustrate the many ways that you can manipulate a table.

1. In this first example, I use the ALTER TABLE statement and the TO keyword to take the Contacts table created earlier and change its name to ContactList.

    ```
    Dim RS As ADOCE.Recordset
    Dim i As Integer
    Set RS = CreateObject("ADOCE.Recordset.3.0")
    RS.Open "ALTER TABLE Contacts TO ContactList", "\My Documents\TestDB.cdb"
    ```

    In the second part of this code, I verify that a table called "ContactList" actually exists by iterating through its fields.

    ```
    RS.Open "ContactList", "\My Documents\TestDB.cdb"
    For i = 0 To RS.Fields.Count - 1
      MsgBox "Field Name: " & RS.Fields(i).Name & vbCrLf & "Data Type: "
    & RS.Fields(i).Type
    Next
    RS.Close
    Set RS = Nothing
    ```

2. In this second example, I use the ALTER TABLE statement with the RENAME keyword to rename the ContactID field as ContactNumber.

    ```
    Dim RS As ADOCE.Recordset
    Dim i As Integer
    Set RS = CreateObject("ADOCE.Recordset.3.0")
    RS.Open "ALTER TABLE ContactList RENAME ContactID TO ContactNumber", "\My
    Documents\TestDB.cdb"
    ```

    In the second part of this code, I verify that the field called "ContactID" has been changed to ContactNumber by iterating through the ContactList fields.

    ```
    RS.Open "ContactList", "\My Documents\TestDB.cdb"
    For i = 0 To RS.Fields.Count - 1
      MsgBox "Field Name: " & RS.Fields(i).Name & vbCrLf & "Data Type: "
    & RS.Fields(i).Type
    ```

```
Next
RS.Close
Set RS = Nothing
```

3. In this third example, I use the ALTER TABLE statement and the ADD keyword to add a new Integer field called "Age."

```
Dim RS As ADOCE.Recordset
Dim i As Integer
Set RS = CreateObject("ADOCE.Recordset.3.0")
RS.Open "ALTER TABLE ContactList ADD Age int BEFORE CompanyName", "\My
Documents\TestDB.cdb"
```

In the second part of this code, I verify that the new field called "Age" has been added and placed before CompanyName by iterating through the ContactList fields.

```
RS.Open "ContactList", "\My Documents\TestDB.cdb"
For i = 0 To RS.Fields.Count - 1
  MsgBox "Field Name: " & RS.Fields(i).Name & vbCrLf & "Data Type: "
& RS.Fields(i).Type
Next
RS.Close
Set RS = Nothing
```

4. In this fourth example, I use the ALTER TABLE statement and the MOVE keyword to position the CompanyName field before the Age field.

```
Dim RS As ADOCE.Recordset
Dim i As Integer
Set RS = CreateObject("ADOCE.Recordset.3.0")
RS.Open "ALTER TABLE ContactList MOVE CompanyName BEFORE Age", "\My
Documents\TestDB.cdb"
```

In the second part of this code, I verify that the CompanyName field has moved in front of the Age field by iterating through the ContactList fields.

```
RS.Open "ContactList", "\My Documents\TestDB.cdb"
For i = 0 To RS.Fields.Count - 1
  MsgBox "Field Name: " & RS.Fields(i).Name & vbCrLf & "Data Type: "
& RS.Fields(i).Type
```

```
Next
RS.Close
Set RS = Nothing
```

5. In this fifth and final example, I use the ALTER TABLE statement and the DROP keyword to delete the Age field from the ContactList table.

```
Dim RS As ADOCE.Recordset
Dim i As Integer
Set RS = CreateObject("ADOCE.Recordset.3.0")
RS.Open "ALTER TABLE ContactList DROP Age", "\My Documents\TestDB.cdb"
Set RS = Nothing
```

In the second part of this code, I verify that the Age field has been deleted by iterating through the ContactList fields.

```
RS.Open "ContactList", "\My Documents\TestDB.cdb"
For i = 0 To RS.Fields.Count - 1
  MsgBox "Field Name: " & RS.Fields(i).Name & vbCrLf & "Data Type: "
& RS.Fields(i).Type
Next
RS.Close
Set RS = Nothing
```

You should now have a new appreciation for the work that Microsoft Access and SQL Server are doing behind the scenes every time you decide to add, move, or change the data type of a field from the convenience of a friendly GUI.

 TIP *For more helpful advice on creating and working with tables, visit http://www.devbuzz.com/content/ primer_CreateTableSql_pg1.asp.*

Deleting a Table

You can delete an existing table in a Pocket Access database with the DROP TABLE statement. The specifics of deleting a table, including the proper statement syntax, an explanation of parameters, the possible return values, and a working example, are as follows.

Syntax

DROP TABLE *TableName*

Parameters

TableName

This is the name of the table to delete.

Return Values

One of the following error values may be returned:

- E_OUTOFMEMORY

- DB_E_ERRORSINCOMMAND

- DB_E_NOTABLE

Example

This simple code deletes the ContactList table using the DROP TABLE statement and an implicit connection to TestDB.cdb:

```
Dim RS As ADOCE.Recordset
Set RS = CreateObject("ADOCE.Recordset.3.0")
RS.Open "DROP TABLE ContactList", "\My Documents\TestDB.cdb"
Set RS = Nothing
```

You can verify that the table no longer exists by using some of the previous code snippets that are designed to open the ContactList table and iterate through its fields. Obviously, you should receive an error message like the one shown in Figure 2-3.

Figure 2-3. An Application Error message

  NOTE *You should know that deleting a table that doesn't exist causes an application error.*

Creating an Index

You can create an index on an existing table in a Pocket Access database with the CREATE INDEX statement. The specifics of creating an index, including the proper statement syntax, an explanation of parameters, the possible return values, and a working example, are as follows.

Syntax

CREATE INDEX *IndexName* ON *TableName* (*FieldName* [DESC]
[CASESENSITIVE] [UNKNOWNFIRST])

Parameters

IndexName

This is the name of the new index.

TableName

This is the name of the table that the index will be created for.

FieldName

This is the name of the field that the index will be created on. Only one field is indexed at a time, and only one index is created per field. You can give the index additional properties by specifying an index attribute after the field name, as described in Table 2-3.

Table 2-3. Index Attributes

INDEX ATTRIBUTE	DESCRIPTION
DESC	This attribute causes the data to be sorted in descending order. Otherwise, data is sorted in ascending order.
CASESENSITIVE	This attribute sorts the capital letters before the lowercase letters. Otherwise, letter sorting is case insensitive.
UNKNOWNFIRST	This attribute sorts the NULL values at the beginning of the table. Otherwise, NULLS are found at the end of the table.

Return Values

One of the following error values may be returned:

- E_OUTOFMEMORY

- DB_E_ERRORSINCOMMAND

- DB_E_DUPLICATEINDEXID

- DB_E_BADCOLUMNID

- DB_E_NOTABLE

Example

In this example, an index called ContactIndex is created on the ContactNumber field in the ContactList database. In this case, no special indexing attributes are used in the statement, so the data is sorted in ascending order.

```
Dim RS As ADOCE.Recordset
Set RS = CreateObject("ADOCE.Recordset.3.0")
RS.Open "CREATE INDEX ContactIndex ON ContactList (ContactNumber)", _
    "\My Documents\TestDB.cdb"
Set RS = Nothing
```

In keeping with the theme of the various Notes in this chapter regarding application errors, the most obvious way to know that an index has been created is to reexecute the previous code snippet where you'll hopefully receive an error stating that an index already exists. The second indicator of an index is that your SELECT statements using both the WHERE and ORDER BY clauses will execute faster. Indexing can sometimes dramatically speed up your database applications and it should never be overlooked in database schema design.

Deleting an Index

In order to delete an index on an existing table in a Pocket Access database, you must use the DROP INDEX statement. The specifics of deleting an index, including the proper statement syntax, an explanation of parameters, the possible return values, and a working example, are as follows.

Syntax

DROP INDEX *TableName. IndexName*

Parameters

TableName

This is the name of the table whose index will be removed.

IndexName

This is the name of the index that will be removed from the table.

Return Values

One of the following error values may be returned:

- E_OUTOFMEMORY

- DB_E_ERRORSINCOMMAND

- DB_E_NOINDEX

- DB_E_NOTABLE

Example

In this example, ContactIndex is removed from the ContactList table.

```
Dim RS As ADOCE.Recordset
Set RS = CreateObject("ADOCE.Recordset.3.0")
RS.Open "DROP INDEX ContactList.ContactIndex", "\My Documents\TestDB.cdb"
Set RS = Nothing
```

As with the example on creating indexes, the best way to verify that your index has been removed is to rerun the preceding code and look for the error message telling you that the index doesn't exist.

Summary

We've reached the end of our discussion on the Pocket SQL Data Definition Language. With just seven different statements to work with, it's fair to call this DDL an understatement. That said, you're now equipped with a foundation you can build upon as you proceed to learn additional aspects of Pocket SQL.

CHAPTER 3

The Pocket SQL Data Manipulation Language

IN CHAPTER 2 YOU LEARNED everything you need to know about building databases, tables, and indexes on the Pocket PC. Now it's time to learn how to make use of those database objects by working with live data. The SQL Data Manipulation Language (DML) describes how data is inserted, updated, retrieved, and deleted. As you're accustomed to hearing by now, the Pocket SQL version of the DML is a limited subset of what you're used to working with on the desktop and the server. The most noticeable limitation is the absence of the UPDATE statement used to modify the values of one or more existing rows in a database. Don't worry, in Chapter 5 I'll show you how to perform updates using Recordset objects. There are many more missing SQL statements that I'm sure you'll feel that you can't live without, but fortunately, all the basics are covered.

Building a Test Database

In order to try out all the forthcoming examples in this Pocket SQL DML reference, you'll need to construct a test database. Luckily for you, Chapter 2 has already shown you the ropes of Pocket DDL, so building this test database will be a breeze. To start, open up eMbedded Visual Basic and create a new project called "DML." Because you're working with a database, go ahead and set a reference to ADOCE. Your single project form will contain three buttons to create a database, create tables, create indexes, delete a database, and view all created fields.

 NOTE *Another way to build a Pocket Access database is to first build a desktop Microsoft Access database using its graphical interface. Chapter 6 explains how you can use ActiveSync to copy that database to your Pocket PC.*

Creating a Database, Tables, and Indexes

Drag a CommandButton from the Toolbox and drop it on your form. Name this control "cmdCreate" and set its caption to read "Create a Database, Tables, and Indexes." In the click event of this CommandButton you'll insert code to create a database, create two tables, and create indexes for those tables. The database you'll create is called "DML.cdb." This database will act as a tiny contact manager and will include a table called "Contacts" and a related table called "PhoneNumbers." Each of the two tables will have a field used to relate them called "ContactID" that will be indexed. The Contacts table includes things like first and last name and fields to capture a full address. Since all these fields are text-based, you use the varchar data type with various lengths. The PhoneNumbers table is used so you won't have any limits on the numbers of phone number you want a given contact to have. This is relational theory 101 at its most basic level. It makes you scratch your head and think back to all the software packages you've used in the past that gave you a fixed amount of phone numbers to associate with a contact because the developer put everything in one table. Anyway, you'll treat the PhoneNumber field like text so you'll use the varchar data type for it. The designs of the two tables are shown in Table 3-1 and Table 3-2.

Table 3-1. The Contacts Table

FIELD NAME	DATE TYPE	INDEXED?	INDEX NAME
ContactID	int	Yes	PrimaryKey
FirstName	varchar(20)	No	
LastName	varchar(20)	No	
CompanyName	varchar(50)	No	
StreetAddress	varchar(50)	No	
City	varchar(20)	No	
State	varchar(2)	No	
Zip	varchar(20)	No	

Table 3-2. The PhoneNumbers Table

FIELD NAME	DATE TYPE	INDEXED?	INDEX NAME
ContactID	int	Yes	Key
PhoneNumber	varchar(12)	No	

In Chapter 2 you learned how to create a database, table, and index using the CREATE DATABASE, CREATE TABLE, and CREATE INDEX DDL statements. To apply what you've learned and to build the database, tables, and indexes all in one shot, add the following code to the click event of cmdCreate:

```
Private Sub cmdCreate_Click()

  cmdCreate.Enabled = False

  'Declare variables
  Dim RS As ADOCE.Recordset
  Dim SQL As String
    Set RS = CreateObject("ADOCE.Recordset.3.0")

  'Create Database
  RS.Open "CREATE DATABASE '\My Documents\DML.cdb'"

  'Create Contacts Table
  SQL = "CREATE TABLE Contacts ("
  SQL = SQL & "ContactID int ,"
  SQL = SQL & "FirstName varchar(20) ,"
  SQL = SQL & "LastName varchar(20) ,"
  SQL = SQL & "CompanyName varchar(50) ,"
  SQL = SQL & "StreetAddress varchar(50) ,"
  SQL = SQL & "City varchar(20) ,"
  SQL = SQL & "State varchar(2) ,"
  SQL = SQL & "Zip varchar(20) )"
  RS.Open SQL, "\My Documents\DML.cdb"

  'Create PhoneNumbers Table
  SQL = "CREATE TABLE PhoneNumbers ("
  SQL = SQL & "ContactID int ,"
  SQL = SQL & "PhoneNumber varchar(12))"
  RS.Open SQL, "\My Documents\DML.cdb"

  'Create Index for Contacts Table
  RS.Open "CREATE INDEX PrimaryKey ON Contacts (ContactID)", _
        "\My Documents\DML.cdb"

  'Create Index for PhoneNumbers Table
  RS.Open "CREATE INDEX Key ON PhoneNumbers (ContactID)", _
        "\My Documents\DML.cdb"
```

```
'Dereference the Recordset
Set RS = Nothing

cmdCreate.Enabled = True

End Sub
```

Viewing Fields

Because you don't yet have a convenient GUI with which to browse tables, fields, and data, you need to build your own. Drag a CommandButton from the Toolbox and drop it on your form. Name this control "cmdViewFields" and set its caption to read "View Fields." In the click event of this CommandButton, you'll insert code to iterate through the two tables and display information about the various fields so you can have instant feedback as to the results of the various database operations you're going to perform.

```
Private Sub cmdViewFields_Click()

  cmdViewFields.Enabled = False

  'Declare Variables
  Dim RSTables As ADOCE.Recordset
  Dim RSFields As ADOCE.Recordset
  Dim RSIndexes As ADOCE.Recordset
  Dim IndexName As String
  Dim FieldID As Integer
  Dim i As Integer
  Dim IndexedFieldName As String
  Dim Indexed As String
  Dim FieldName As String
  Dim FieldType As String
  Dim FieldValue As String
  Dim TableID As Integer
  Dim TableName As String
  Set RSTables = CreateObject("ADOCE.Recordset.3.0")
  Set RSFields = CreateObject("ADOCE.Recordset.3.0")
  Set RSIndexes = CreateObject("ADOCE.Recordset.3.0")

  'View all Tables in Database
  RSTables.Open "MSysTables", "\My Documents\DML.cdb"
```

```
While Not RSTables.EOF

  'Disregard all System Tables
  If RSTables("TableName") <> "MSysTables" _
  And RSTables("TableName") <> "MSysIndexes" _
  And RSTables("TableName") <> "MSysFields" _
  And RSTables("TableName") <> "MSysProcs" Then

    'Get the Table ID and Table Name
    TableID = RSTables("TableID")
    TableName = RSTables("TableName")

    'View all Indexes
    RSIndexes.Open "MSysIndexes", "\My Documents\DML.cdb"
    While Not RSIndexes.EOF

      'Only look at Indexes in the current table
      If RSIndexes("TableID") = TableID Then
        IndexName = RSIndexes("IndexName")
        FieldID = RSIndexes("FieldID")

        'View all Fields looking for the indexed fields
        RSFields.Open "MSysFields", "\My Documents\DML.cdb"
        While Not RSFields.EOF

          If RSFields("FieldID") = FieldID And RSFields("TableID") = TableID Then
            IndexedFieldName = RSFields("FieldName")
          End If
          RSFields.MoveNext
        Wend
        RSFields.Close

      End If
      RSIndexes.MoveNext
    Wend
    RSIndexes.Close

    'View all Fields in Table
    RSFields.Open TableName, "\My Documents\DML.cdb"
    For i = 0 To RSFields.Fields.Count - 1

      'Convert the Field Type number
```

```
        'into a meaningful string
        Select Case RSFields.Fields(i).Type
          Case 202
            FieldType = "Varchar"
          Case 203
            FieldType = "Text"
          Case 204
            FieldType = "Varbinary"
          Case 205
            FieldType = "Long Varbinary"
          Case 3
            FieldType = "Integer"
          Case 2
            FieldType = "Smallint"
          Case 5
            FieldType = "Float"
          Case 7
            FieldType = "Datetime"
          Case 11
            FieldType = "Bit"
        End Select

        'Get the Field Name
        FieldName = RSFields.Fields(i).Name

        'If there is data in the table
        'then get the Field Value
        If Not RSFields.EOF And Not RSFields.BOF Then
          FieldValue = RSFields.Fields(i).Value
        Else
          FieldValue = ""
        End If

        If FieldName = IndexedFieldName Then
          Indexed = "Yes"

          'Display the Data
          MsgBox "Table Name: " & RSTables("TableName") & vbCrLf _
          & "Field Name: " & FieldName & vbCrLf _
          & "Data Type:  " & FieldType & vbCrLf _
          & "Field Value: " & FieldValue & vbCrLf _
          & "Indexed:    " & Indexed & vbCrLf _
```

```
                & "Index Name: " & IndexName

          Else
            Indexed = "No"

            'Display the Data
            MsgBox "Table Name: " & RSTables("TableName") & vbCrLf _
            & "Field Name: " & FieldName & vbCrLf _
            & "Data Type:  " & FieldType & vbCrLf _
            & "Field Value: " & FieldValue & vbCrLf _
            & "Indexed:    " & Indexed

        End If
      Next
      RSFields.Close

    End If
    RSTables.MoveNext
  Wend
  RSTables.Close

  'Dereference the Recordsets
  Set RSTables = Nothing
  Set RSFields = Nothing
  Set RSIndexes = Nothing

  cmdViewFields.Enabled = True

End Sub
```

In the previous block of code, you found yourself opening Recordsets against unfamiliar system tables in the Pocket PC object store. The MSysTables table contains metadata about every table in your database as well as the object store. The MSysIndexes table contains metadata about all the indexes in your database and those in the object store. Finally, the MSysFields table contains metadata about all the fields in your database along with the fields in the object store. By iterating through these system tables as well as the tables in the DML database, you can view the same kind of information that would normally be displayed in the Microsoft Access table designer. I'm sure you'll find the View Fields button a handy thing to have around throughout the rest of this chapter to verify that the upcoming examples manipulate data correctly. Running a quick test of the View Fields code should reveal something that looks like Figure 3-1.

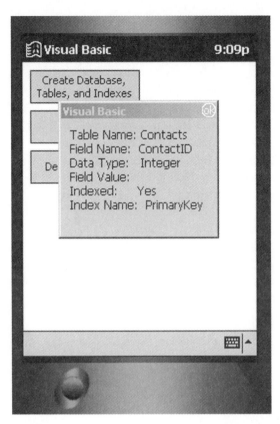

Figure 3-1. The message boxes that result from clicking View Fields

NOTE *The Windows CE object store is the persistent storage that it makes available to applications. Windows CE reserves part of its available memory for the operating system and uses the rest for the object store. The object store data can be stored in files, registry entries, or in Windows CE databases.*

Deleting a Database

In Chapter 2, you learned how to delete a database using the DROP DATABASE DDL statement. It's now time to apply that know-how. Drag a CommandButton from the Toolbox and drop it on your form. Name this control "cmdDelete" and set its caption to read "Delete Database." In the click event of this CommandButton, insert the now-familiar code to delete the database.

```
Private Sub cmdDelete_Click()

  cmdDelete.Enabled = False

  Dim RS As ADOCE.Recordset
  Set RS = CreateObject("ADOCE.Recordset.3.0")
  RS.Open "DROP DATABASE '\My Documents\DML.cdb'"

  'Dereference the Recordset
  Set RS = Nothing

  cmdDelete.Enabled = True

End Sub
```

Now that you have the necessary DDL code in place to build, view, and delete your database and tables, you can start filling those tables with data.

Inserting Data

You can add a new row of data into a table by using the INSERT INTO statement. The insertion of complete or partial rows into a table is possible. You can either choose to name the columns you wish to insert data into, or you may omit them as long as your data is in proper comma-delimited order. I recommend that you name your columns just in case they get rearranged in the table. Also, your code will be easier for others to maintain because it is easier to see where the data is going when the column names are referenced. If you want to insert only a portion of your data, name the columns and provide the associated data for the subset of fields you want to populate.

Syntax

INSERT INTO *TableName* [(*ColumnName*, . . .)] VALUES (*Constant*, . . .)

Parameters

TableName

This is the name of the table that the data is inserted into.

ColumnName

This specifies the name of the field where data is stored.

Constant

This specifies the data that will be stored in the fields.

Return Values

None.

Example

In this example, you'll create SQL statements that use the INSERT INTO statement to add data to both the Contacts and PhoneNumbers tables. Drag a CommandButton from the Toolbox and drop it on your form. Name this control "cmdInsert" and set its caption to read "Insert Data." In the click event of this CommandButton, insert the following code:

```
Private Sub cmdInsert_Click()

  cmdInsert.Enabled = False

  'Declare Variables
  Dim RS As ADOCE.Recordset
  Dim SQL As String
  Set RS = CreateObject("ADOCE.Recordset.3.0")

  'Create SQL Insert Statement
  'for Contact #1 in the Contacts Table
  SQL = "INSERT INTO Contacts ("
  SQL = SQL & "ContactID, "
  SQL = SQL & "FirstName, "
  SQL = SQL & "LastName, "
  SQL = SQL & "CompanyName, "
  SQL = SQL & "StreetAddress, "
  SQL = SQL & "City, "
  SQL = SQL & "State, "
  SQL = SQL & "Zip) "
  SQL = SQL & "VALUES ("
```

```
SQL = SQL & "1, "
SQL = SQL & "'Rob', "
SQL = SQL & "'Tiffany', "
SQL = SQL & "'Apress', "
SQL = SQL & "'123 Elm St', "
SQL = SQL & "'Houston', "
SQL = SQL & "'TX', "
SQL = SQL & "12345)"
RS.Open SQL, "\My Documents\DML.cdb"


'Create 2 SQL Insert Statements
'for Contact #1 in the PhoneNumbers Table
SQL = "INSERT INTO PhoneNumbers ("
SQL = SQL & "ContactID, "
SQL = SQL & "PhoneNumber) "
SQL = SQL & "VALUES ("
SQL = SQL & "1, "
SQL = SQL & "'713-123-4567')"
RS.Open SQL, "\My Documents\DML.cdb"


SQL = "INSERT INTO PhoneNumbers ("
SQL = SQL & "ContactID, "
SQL = SQL & "PhoneNumber) "
SQL = SQL & "VALUES ("
SQL = SQL & "1, "
SQL = SQL & "'281-123-4567')"
RS.Open SQL, "\My Documents\DML.cdb"


'Create SQL Insert Statement
'for Contact #2 in the Contacts Table
SQL = "INSERT INTO Contacts ("
SQL = SQL & "ContactID, "
SQL = SQL & "FirstName, "
SQL = SQL & "LastName, "
SQL = SQL & "CompanyName, "
SQL = SQL & "StreetAddress, "
SQL = SQL & "City, "
SQL = SQL & "State, "
SQL = SQL & "Zip) "
SQL = SQL & "VALUES ("
SQL = SQL & "2, "
SQL = SQL & "'Mark', "
SQL = SQL & "'Hoben', "
```

```
SQL = SQL & "'Met Travel', "
SQL = SQL & "'321 Rainy St', "
SQL = SQL & "'Seattle', "
SQL = SQL & "'WA', "
SQL = SQL & "54321)"
RS.Open SQL, "\My Documents\DML.cdb"

'Create 2 SQL Insert Statements
'for Contact #2 in the PhoneNumbers Table
SQL = "INSERT INTO PhoneNumbers ("
SQL = SQL & "ContactID, "
SQL = SQL & "PhoneNumber) "
SQL = SQL & "VALUES ("
SQL = SQL & "2, "
SQL = SQL & "'206-123-4567')"
RS.Open SQL, "\My Documents\DML.cdb"

SQL = "INSERT INTO PhoneNumbers ("
SQL = SQL & "ContactID, "
SQL = SQL & "PhoneNumber) "
SQL = SQL & "VALUES ("
SQL = SQL & "2, "
SQL = SQL & "'425-123-4567')"
RS.Open SQL, "\My Documents\DML.cdb"

'Create SQL Insert Statement
'for Contact #3 in the Contacts Table
SQL = "INSERT INTO Contacts ("
SQL = SQL & "ContactID, "
SQL = SQL & "FirstName, "
SQL = SQL & "LastName, "
SQL = SQL & "CompanyName, "
SQL = SQL & "StreetAddress, "
SQL = SQL & "City, "
SQL = SQL & "State, "
SQL = SQL & "Zip) "
SQL = SQL & "VALUES ("
SQL = SQL & "3, "
SQL = SQL & "'Jeff', "
SQL = SQL & "'Swantkowski', "
SQL = SQL & "'Kanaly Trust', "
SQL = SQL & "'987 Money Ave', "
SQL = SQL & "'Houston', "
```

```
SQL = SQL & "'TX', "
SQL = SQL & "98765)"
RS.Open SQL, "\My Documents\DML.cdb"

'Create 2 SQL Insert Statements
'for Contact #3 in the PhoneNumbers Table
SQL = "INSERT INTO PhoneNumbers ("
SQL = SQL & "ContactID, "
SQL = SQL & "PhoneNumber) "
SQL = SQL & "VALUES ("
SQL = SQL & "3, "
SQL = SQL & "'713-987-6543')"
RS.Open SQL, "\My Documents\DML.cdb"

SQL = "INSERT INTO PhoneNumbers ("
SQL = SQL & "ContactID, "
SQL = SQL & "PhoneNumber) "
SQL = SQL & "VALUES ("
SQL = SQL & "3, "
SQL = SQL & "'281-987-6543')"
RS.Open SQL, "\My Documents\DML.cdb"

'Dereference the Recordset
Set RS = Nothing

cmdInsert.Enabled = True

End Sub
```

Feel free to change the code to insert the names and phone numbers of your friends instead of mine. You now have plenty of data to work with for the rest of the chapter. While the syntax for the previous data inserts look pretty normal, you may be asking yourself why you aren't using an identity/autonumber field for your ContactID unique index. The unfortunate answer is that Pocket Access doesn't support an autonumber column. To make matters worse, the MAX function isn't supported by ADOCE either, so there goes that autoincrementing workaround idea as well. I'll provide a workaround that you can use on the Pocket PC when I discuss how to sort data later in this chapter.

Retrieving Data

You can retrieve data from a table with the SELECT statement. Data can be retrieved from all columns without having to name them by using the SELECT statement in conjunction with an asterisk (*). Alternatively, listing the desired fields separated by commas can return specific columns.

Syntax

SELECT [*] [*TableName.*] *FieldName* [, [*TableName.*] *FieldName* . . .] FROM *TableName*

Parameters

TableName

This is the name of the table that you'll be retrieving data from.

FieldName

This is the name of the field to include in the Recordset.

Return Values

None.

Examples

In order to properly visualize the retrieval of data from your new database, it's useful to display the data in a grid on your form. Go to the embedded Visual Basic menu, select Project ➤ Components, check the Microsoft CE Grid Control 3.0 option, and then click OK. Now drag the Grid control from the Toolbox and drop it on your form. Go to the Properties of the Grid control and set Cols equal to 8 and Rows equal to 0. You will use this Grid control in all of the remaining examples in this chapter.

Retrieve All Columns

In this first example, you'll use the simple SELECT statement with the * in order to return all the columns from the Contacts table. Drag a CommandButton from the Toolbox and drop it on your form. Name this control "cmdRetrieve" and set its caption to read "Retrieve All Columns." In the click event of this Command-Button, insert the following code:

```
Private Sub cmdRetrieve_Click()

  cmdRetrieve.Enabled = False

  'Declare Variables
  Dim RS As ADOCE.Recordset
  Dim SQL As String
  Dim i As Integer
  Set RS = CreateObject("ADOCE.Recordset.3.0")

  'Build Simple SELECT statement to return all fields
  SQL = "SELECT * FROM Contacts"
  RS.Open SQL, "\My Documents\DML.cdb"

  'Remove existing data from Grid
  For i = 1 To GridCtrl1.Rows
    GridCtrl1.RemoveItem 0
  Next

  'Populate column headers
  GridCtrl1.AddItem "ContactID" & vbTab & _
                    "FirstName" & vbTab & _
                    "LastName" & vbTab & _
                    "CompanyName" & vbTab & _
                    "StreetAddress" & vbTab & _
                    "City" & vbTab & _
                    "State" & vbTab & _
                    "Zip"

  'Loop through Recordset to populate Grid
  While Not RS.EOF
    GridCtrl1.AddItem RS("ContactID") & vbTab & _
                      RS("FirstName") & vbTab & _
                      RS("LastName") & vbTab & _
```

```
                              RS("CompanyName") & vbTab & _
                              RS("StreetAddress") & vbTab & _
                              RS("City") & vbTab & _
                              RS("State") & vbTab & _
                              RS("Zip")
        RS.MoveNext
    Wend
    RS.Close

    'Dereference the Recordset
    Set RS = Nothing

    cmdRetrieve.Enabled = True

End Sub
```

If your code executed correctly, your Grid should look something like the one you see in Figure 3-2.

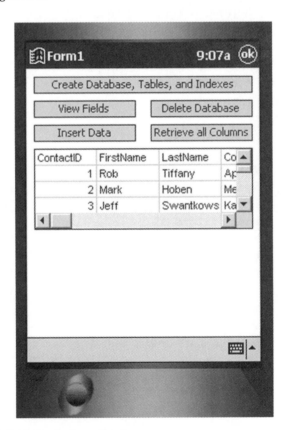

Figure 3-2. A Grid displaying all columns

NOTE *Data is added to the Grid control using the AddItem method. Additionally, all items added to each of the Grid columns must be separated by vbTab. Data is removed from the Grid using the RemoveItem method. Clearing out an entire Grid is accomplished by looping through all the Grid's rows and removing the zero index row each time.*

Retrieve Selected Columns

In this next example, you'll use the SELECT statement combined with field names to return only selected columns from the Contacts table. Drag a CommandButton from the Toolbox and drop it on your form. Name this control "cmdRetrieveSelected" and set its caption to read "Retrieve Selected Columns." In the click event of this CommandButton, insert the following code:

```
Private Sub cmdRetrieveSelected_Click()

  cmdRetrieveSelected.Enabled = False

  'Declare Variables
  Dim RS As ADOCE.Recordset
  Dim SQL As String
  Dim i As Integer
  Set RS = CreateObject("ADOCE.Recordset.3.0")

  'Build SELECT statement to return selected fields
  SQL = "SELECT FirstName, LastName, City FROM Contacts"
  RS.Open SQL, "\My Documents\DML.cdb"

  'Remove existing data from Grid
  For i = 1 To GridCtrl1.Rows
    GridCtrl1.RemoveItem 0
  Next

  'Populate column headers
  GridCtrl1.AddItem "FirstName" & vbTab & _
                    "LastName" & vbTab & _
                    "City"
```

```
'Loop through Recordset to populate Grid
While Not RS.EOF
  GridCtrl1.AddItem RS("FirstName") & vbTab & _
                    RS("LastName") & vbTab & _
                    RS("City")
  RS.MoveNext
Wend
RS.Close

'Dereference the Recordset
Set RS = Nothing

cmdRetrieveSelected.Enabled = True

End Sub
```

If your code executed correctly, your Grid should look something like the one you see in Figure 3-3.

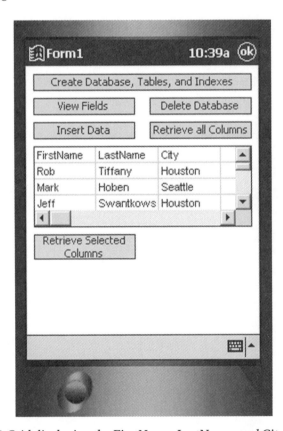

Figure 3-3. A Grid displaying the FirstName, LastName, and City columns

To reinforce what you've learned through this code example, try plugging in various combinations of column names and view the results in the Grid.

Filtering Data

Tables often contain large amounts of data, and rarely do you want to return every row. You can retrieve a subset of rows from one or more tables by using the WHERE clause in conjunction with the SELECT statement. Using a multitude of operators and expressions, the WHERE clause provides a powerful filter for displaying reports.

Syntax

SELECT * FROM *TableName* WHERE *FieldNameExpression* [AND|OR *FieldName-Expression*]

Parameters

TableName

This is the name of the table that you'll be retrieving data from.

FieldNameExpression

This can take one of the following forms:

- [NOT] FieldName Operator Constant

- FieldName IS [NOT] NULL

- FieldName IS [NOT] TRUE

- FieldName IS [NOT] FALSE

- FieldName [NOT] LIKE "STRING%"

The FieldName is the name of the column in the table that's used in a comparison operation. A Constant can be a number, string, or date enclosed by quotation marks. String Constants that use the percent (%) wildcard character are covered in the Pattern Matching section later in this chapter.

The creamy filling found between the FieldName and the Constant in a Where clause is the Operator. Table 3-3 displays a selection of Operators that are available to you.

Table 3-3. Operator Options

OPERATOR	DESCRIPTION
=	Equal to
>	Greater than
>=	Greater than or equal to
<	Less than
<=	Less than or equal to
<>	Not equal to

 TIP *Because the BETWEEN clause isn't supported by ADOCE, use the WHERE clause in conjunction with the greater than and less than operators.*

Return Values

One of the following error values may be returned:

- E_OUTOFMEMORY

- DB_E_ERRORSINCOMMAND

- DB_E_NOTABLE

- DB_E_BADCOLUMNID

- DB_E_CANTCONVERTVALUE

- DB_E_DATAOVERFLOW

Example

In this example, you'll continue to use the Grid control to display the results of using the equal to operator in combination with the WHERE clause to return rows where the State column is equal to TX from the Contacts table. Drag a

CommandButton from the Toolbox and drop it on your form. Name this control "cmdEqualTo" and set its caption to read "WHERE Equal To." In the click event of this CommandButton, insert the following code:

```
Private Sub cmdEqualTo_Click()

  cmdEqualTo.Enabled = False

  'Declare Variables
  Dim RS As ADOCE.Recordset
  Dim SQL As String
  Dim i As Integer
  Set RS = CreateObject("ADOCE.Recordset.3.0")

  'Build SELECT statement to return all rows where the state columns equals TX
  SQL = "SELECT * FROM Contacts WHERE State = 'TX'"
  RS.Open SQL, "\My Documents\DML.cdb"

  'Remove existing data from Grid
  For i = 1 To GridCtrl1.Rows
    GridCtrl1.RemoveItem 0
  Next

  'Populate column headers
  GridCtrl1.AddItem "ContactID" & vbTab & _
                    "FirstName" & vbTab & _
                    "LastName" & vbTab & _
                    "CompanyName" & vbTab & _
                    "StreetAddress" & vbTab & _
                    "City" & vbTab & _
                    "State" & vbTab & _
                    "Zip"

  'Loop through Recordset to populate Grid
  While Not RS.EOF
    GridCtrl1.AddItem RS("ContactID") & vbTab & _
                      RS("FirstName") & vbTab & _
                      RS("LastName") & vbTab & _
                      RS("CompanyName") & vbTab & _
                      RS("StreetAddress") & vbTab & _
                      RS("City") & vbTab & _
                      RS("State") & vbTab & _
                      RS("Zip")
```

```
        RS.MoveNext
     Wend
     RS.Close

     'Dereference the Recordset
     Set RS = Nothing

     cmdEqualTo.Enabled = True

End Sub
```

If your code executed correctly, your Grid should look something like the one you see in Figure 3-4.

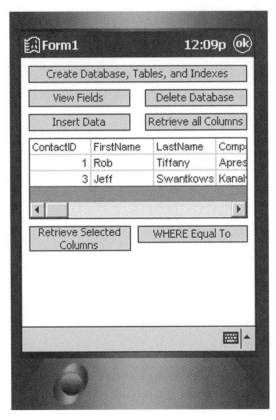

Figure 3-4. A Grid displaying rows where the State column is equal to TX

Shake things up a bit in this code example by using the <> operator to see how your results differ. Go even further by substituting column name expressions other than State.

Sorting Data

When you retrieve data from a table, it may appear that the data is returned in no particular order. Data is actually retrieved in the order in which it appears in the table. You can sort specific columns in the data you're retrieving by using the ORDER BY clause in conjunction with the SELECT statement. One or more columns may be sorted, and that sort order may be ascending, which is the default, or descending.

Syntax

SELECT * FROM *TableName* ORDER BY *FieldName* [*ASC* | *DESC*]

Parameters

TableName

This is the name of the table that you'll be retrieving data from.

FieldName

This is the name of the field used to sort the rows.

Return Values

One of the following error values may be returned:

- E_OUTOFMEMORY

- DB_E_ERRORSINCOMMAND

- DB_E_NOTABLE

- DB_E_BADCOLUMNID

Examples

1. In this first example, I'll show you how to use the ORDER BY clause against the unindexed field, LastName. Drag a CommandButton from the Toolbox and drop it on your form. Name this control "cmdOrderBy" and set its caption to read "Order By LastName." In the click event of this CommandButton, insert the following code:

```
Private Sub cmdOrderBy_Click()

  cmdOrderBy.Enabled = False

  'Declare Variables
  Dim RS As ADOCE.Recordset
  Dim SQL As String
  Dim i As Integer
  Set RS = CreateObject("ADOCE.Recordset.3.0")

  'Build Simple SELECT statement to return rows ordered by LastName
  SQL = "SELECT * FROM Contacts ORDER BY LastName ASC"
  RS.Open SQL, "\My Documents\DML.cdb"

  'Remove existing data from Grid
  For i = 1 To GridCtrl1.Rows
    GridCtrl1.RemoveItem 0
  Next

  'Populate column headers
  GridCtrl1.AddItem "ContactID" & vbTab & _
                    "FirstName" & vbTab & _
                    "LastName" & vbTab & _
                    "CompanyName" & vbTab & _
                    "StreetAddress" & vbTab & _
                    "City" & vbTab & _
                    "State" & vbTab & _
                    "Zip"

  'Loop through Recordset to populate Grid
  While Not RS.EOF
    GridCtrl1.AddItem RS("ContactID") & vbTab & _
                      RS("FirstName") & vbTab & _
                      RS("LastName") & vbTab & _
```

```
                        RS("CompanyName") & vbTab & _
                        RS("StreetAddress") & vbTab & _
                        RS("City") & vbTab & _
                        RS("State") & vbTab & _
                        RS("Zip")
        RS.MoveNext
    Wend
    RS.Close

    'Dereference the Recordset
    Set RS = Nothing

    cmdOrderBy.Enabled = True

End Sub
```

If your code executed correctly, your Grid should look something like the
one you see in Figure 3-5.

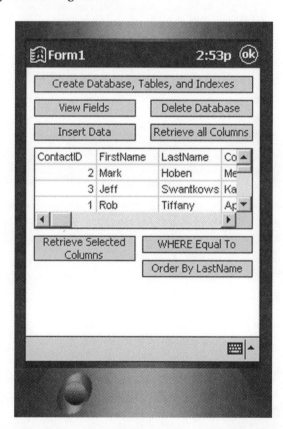

Figure 3-5. A Grid displaying rows that have been sorted by LastName

Enhance your comprehension of the ORDER BY clause by using it against other column names.

2. Earlier in the chapter, I mentioned that Pocket Access databases don't support autoincrementing key fields. The problem is that many times you need a primary key column comprised of unique numbers that increment every time you add a new row to the table. These are the numbers that foreign key fields in related tables need to match up with in order for you to perform table lookups. Using the ORDER BY clause, I'll show you the workaround for this problem. By default, the ORDER BY clause returns data in A to Z ascending order. By using the optional DESC keyword in the ORDER BY clause against your primary key field, you can return those values in Z to A descending order. Using this strategy, you can ensure that the first record returned from this query will be the largest ContactID number. You then add 1 to the returned number to generate the next number in the sequence to use when inserting new data. This strategy is shown in the following code:

```
Private Sub cmdAutoIncrement_Click()

  cmdOrderBy.Enabled = False

  'Declare Variables
  Dim RS As ADOCE.Recordset
  Dim SQL As String
  Dim i As Integer
  Dim AutoNumber As Integer
  Set RS = CreateObject("ADOCE.Recordset.3.0")

  'Build SELECT statement to return rows in reverse order by ContactID
  SQL = "SELECT ContactID FROM Contacts ORDER BY ContactID DESC"
  RS.Open SQL, "\My Documents\DML.cdb"
  AutoNumber = CInt(RS(0)) + 1
  RS.Close

  'Display the newly incremented ContactID number
  MsgBox "New ContactID Number: " & AutoNumber

  'Create SQL Insert Statement
  'for new Contact in the Contacts Table
  SQL = "INSERT INTO Contacts ("
  SQL = SQL & "ContactID, "
```

```
SQL = SQL & "FirstName, "
SQL = SQL & "LastName, "
SQL = SQL & "CompanyName, "
SQL = SQL & "StreetAddress, "
SQL = SQL & "City, "
SQL = SQL & "State, "
SQL = SQL & "Zip) "
SQL = SQL & "VALUES ("
SQL = SQL & AutoNumber & ", "
SQL = SQL & "'Peter', "
SQL = SQL & "'Sutter', "
SQL = SQL & "'SMI', "
SQL = SQL & "'123 Wilshire', "
SQL = SQL & "'Los Angeles', "
SQL = SQL & "'CA', "
SQL = SQL & "90210)"
RS.Open SQL, "\My Documents\DML.cdb"


'Create 2 SQL Insert Statements
'for new Contact in the PhoneNumbers Table
SQL = "INSERT INTO PhoneNumbers ("
SQL = SQL & "ContactID, "
SQL = SQL & "PhoneNumber) "
SQL = SQL & "VALUES ("
SQL = SQL & AutoNumber & ", "
SQL = SQL & "'310-123-4567')"
RS.Open SQL, "\My Documents\DML.cdb"


SQL = "INSERT INTO PhoneNumbers ("
SQL = SQL & "ContactID, "
SQL = SQL & "PhoneNumber) "
SQL = SQL & "VALUES ("
SQL = SQL & AutoNumber & ", "
SQL = SQL & "'323-123-4567')"
RS.Open SQL, "\My Documents\DML.cdb"


'Build Simple SELECT statement to return all fields
SQL = "SELECT * FROM Contacts"
RS.Open SQL, "\My Documents\DML.cdb"


'Remove existing data from Grid
For i = 1 To GridCtrl1.Rows
  GridCtrl1.RemoveItem 0
Next
```

```
          'Populate column headers
          GridCtrl1.AddItem "ContactID" & vbTab & _
                            "FirstName" & vbTab & _
                            "LastName" & vbTab & _
                            "CompanyName" & vbTab & _
                            "StreetAddress" & vbTab & _
                            "City" & vbTab & _
                            "State" & vbTab & _
                            "Zip"

          'Loop through Recordset to populate Grid
          While Not RS.EOF
            GridCtrl1.AddItem RS("ContactID") & vbTab & _
                              RS("FirstName") & vbTab & _
                              RS("LastName") & vbTab & _
                              RS("CompanyName") & vbTab & _
                              RS("StreetAddress") & vbTab & _
                              RS("City") & vbTab & _
                              RS("State") & vbTab & _
                              RS("Zip")
            RS.MoveNext
          Wend
          RS.Close

          'Dereference the Recordset
          Set RS = Nothing

          cmdAutoIncrement.Enabled = True

        End Sub
```

If your code executed correctly, your Grid should look something like the one you see in Figure 3-6.

Figure 3-6. A Grid displaying a new row based on the AutoNumber field

In case you're wondering what AutoNumber = CInt(RS(0)) + 1 means, I'll break it down to make it more understandable. The first column of a Recordset can be accessed using RS(0) to denote the zero index of the column array rather than specifying a column name. The CInt function ensures that the column value is returned as an Integer. You then add 1 and set everything equal to your AutoNumber variable.

Pattern Matching

When you want to retrieve data that matches a particular pattern from a table, you can use the LIKE operator in conjunction with the percent sign (%) wildcard character, the WHERE clause, and the SELECT statement. Finding data within other data is a powerful filtering tool. You can search for this data at the beginning, middle, or end of a string using the percent (%) wildcard character.

Syntax

SELECT * FROM *TableName* WHERE *MatchExpression* [NOT] LIKE *Pattern*

Parameters

TableName

This is the name of the table that you're retrieving data from.

MatchExpression

This is the string SQL expression to compare with the pattern.

Pattern

This is the pattern to search for in the MatchExpression parameter that may contain the percent character (%) as a wildcard. Table 3–4 displays the three ways you can use the wildcard character with the LIKE operator.

Table 3-4. Wildcard Character (%) String Search Patterns

TYPE OF SEARCH	WILDCARD PATTERN
String begins with 'type'	LIKE 'type%'
String contains 'type'	LIKE '%type%'
String ends with 'type'	LIKE '%type'

Return Values

None.

Example

In this example, you'll use the Grid control to display the results of using the LIKE operator in combination with the WHERE clause to return rows where the City column is LIKE Angel from the Contacts table. Drag a CommandButton from the Toolbox and drop it on your form. Name this control "cmdPattern" and set its caption to read "Pattern Matching." In the click event of this CommandButton, insert the following code:

```
Private Sub cmdPattern_Click()

  cmdPattern.Enabled = False

  'Declare Variables
  Dim RS As ADOCE.Recordset
  Dim SQL As String
  Dim i As Integer
  Set RS = CreateObject("ADOCE.Recordset.3.0")

  'Build Simple SELECT statement to return all row that equal TX
  SQL = "SELECT * FROM Contacts WHERE City LIKE '%Angel%'"
  RS.Open SQL, "\My Documents\DML.cdb"

  'Remove existing data from Grid
  For i = 1 To GridCtrl1.Rows
    GridCtrl1.RemoveItem 0
  Next

  'Populate column headers
  GridCtrl1.AddItem "ContactID" & vbTab & _
                    "FirstName" & vbTab & _
                    "LastName" & vbTab & _
                    "CompanyName" & vbTab & _
                    "StreetAddress" & vbTab & _
                    "City" & vbTab & _
                    "State" & vbTab & _
                    "Zip"

  'Loop through Recordset to populate Grid
  While Not RS.EOF
    GridCtrl1.AddItem RS("ContactID") & vbTab & _
                      RS("FirstName") & vbTab & _
                      RS("LastName") & vbTab & _
                      RS("CompanyName") & vbTab & _
                      RS("StreetAddress") & vbTab & _
                      RS("City") & vbTab & _
                      RS("State") & vbTab & _
                      RS("Zip")
    RS.MoveNext
  Wend
  RS.Close
```

```
'Dereference the Recordset
Set RS = Nothing

cmdPattern.Enabled = True

End Sub
```

If your code executed correctly, your Grid should look something like the one you see in Figure 3-7.

Figure 3-7. A Grid displaying the results of using the LIKE statement

See what happens in your code when you use different expressions with the LIKE operator. Try using different wildcard patterns.

Joining Tables

You can combine data retrieval from multiple tables with commonly named columns that are equivalent to each other by using the INNER JOIN clause and the ON operator in conjunction with the SELECT statement. Your results can be further restricted using the WHERE clause. You can also sort the combined result using the ORDER BY clause.

Syntax

SELECT [*TableName1.*] *FieldName1* [, [*TableName2.*] *FieldName2* . . .]

FROM *TableName1*

INNER JOIN *TableName2*

ON *TableName1.FieldName1* = *TableName2.FieldName2*

NOTE *When you execute a query against two or more tables that contain columns with the same name, put the table name and a dot (.) immediately in front of the column names.*

Parameters

TableName

This is the name of the table that you're retrieving data from.

FieldName

This is the name of the field to include in the Recordset.

Return Values

None.

Example

In this example, you'll use the Grid control to first display the results of the simple SELECT query you used earlier in the chapter. Then you'll add code to the Grid's click event to execute your INNER JOIN query based on the ContactID of the row you clicked. The result of this query will be the related phone numbers associated with the ContactID of the row you clicked. You'll then fill a ListBox with the resulting phone numbers. To get started, drag a Label from the Toolbox and drop it on your form. Set its caption to read "Phone Numbers." Now drag a ListBox from the Toolbox and drop it on your form underneath the label. In the click event of the Grid, insert the following code:

```
Private Sub GridCtrl1_Click()

  'Declare Variables
  Dim RS As ADOCE.Recordset
  Dim SQL As String
  Dim i As Integer
  Dim KeyField As Integer
  Set RS = CreateObject("ADOCE.Recordset.3.0")

  'Ensure that the following code is executed
  'only if the user clicks a valid nonheader row.
  If GridCtrl1.RowSel > 0 Then

    'Return the data found in the cell at the intersection
    'of the selected row and column 0 to get the ContactID
    KeyField = GridCtrl1.TextMatrix(GridCtrl1.RowSel, 0)

    'Build INNER JOIN SELECT statement to return the
    'PhoneNumber rows associated with a given KeyField
    SQL = "SELECT PhoneNumbers.PhoneNumber "
    SQL = SQL & "FROM Contacts INNER JOIN PhoneNumbers "
    SQL = SQL & "ON Contacts.ContactID = PhoneNumbers.ContactID "
    SQL = SQL & "WHERE Contacts.ContactID = " & KeyField
    RS.Open SQL, "\My Documents\DML.cdb"

    'Remove existing data from listbox
    List1.Clear
```

```
'Loop through Recordset to populate listbox
While Not RS.EOF
  List1.AddItem RS("PhoneNumber")
  RS.MoveNext
Wend
RS.Close

'Dereference the Recordset
Set RS = Nothing

  End If

End Sub
```

If your code executed correctly, your Grid should look something like the one you see in Figure 3-8.

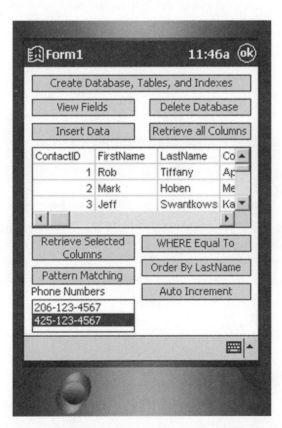

Figure 3-8. Phone numbers displayed as a result of clicking the Grid

NOTE *Unlike the Grid, you can remove all the data from a ListBox using the Clear method. Using the Clear method removes the data, but it doesn't remove the empty rows.*

Deleting Data

You can delete one or more rows of data from a table by using the DELETE statement. When you want to specify the rows to delete, you must use the WHERE clause. You can delete the entire table if you don't use the WHERE clause. You should take great care when you use the DELETE statement because the database won't let you undo the operation once it's complete.

Syntax

DELETE [FROM] *TableName* [WHERE *WhereExpression*]

Parameters

TableName

This is the name of the table where the rows are deleted.

WhereExpression

When this WHERE clause expression is used, only the rows that match this expression are deleted.

Return Values

- E_OUTOFMEMORY

- DB_E_ERRORSINCOMMAND

- DB_E_NOTABLE

- DB_E_BADCOLUMNID

- DB_E_CANTCONVERTVALUE

- DB_E_DATAOVERFLOW

Example

In this example, you'll use the Grid control to display the remaining rows in the table after you've executed a DELETE query to remove everything from Texas. Drag a CommandButton from the Toolbox and drop it on your form. Set its name to "cmdDeleteRows" and set its caption to read "Delete Rows." In the click event of this CommandButton, insert the following code:

```
Private Sub cmdDeleteRows_Click()

  cmdDeleteRows.Enabled = False

  'Declare Variables
  Dim RS As ADOCE.Recordset
  Dim SQL As String
  Dim i As Integer
  Set RS = CreateObject("ADOCE.Recordset.3.0")

  'Build DELETE statement to remove rows
  'where the state is TX
  SQL = "DELETE Contacts WHERE State = 'TX'"
  RS.Open SQL, "\My Documents\DML.cdb"

  'Build Simple SELECT statement to return all fields
  SQL = "SELECT * FROM Contacts"
  RS.Open SQL, "\My Documents\DML.cdb"

  'Remove existing data from Grid
  For i = 1 To GridCtrl1.Rows
    GridCtrl1.RemoveItem 0
  Next
```

```
'Populate column headers
GridCtrl1.AddItem "ContactID" & vbTab & _
                 "FirstName" & vbTab & _
                 "LastName" & vbTab & _
                 "CompanyName" & vbTab & _
                 "StreetAddress" & vbTab & _
                 "City" & vbTab & _
                 "State" & vbTab & _
                 "Zip"

'Loop through Recordset to populate Grid
While Not RS.EOF
  GridCtrl1.AddItem RS("ContactID") & vbTab & _
                    RS("FirstName") & vbTab & _
                    RS("LastName") & vbTab & _
                    RS("CompanyName") & vbTab & _
                    RS("StreetAddress") & vbTab & _
                    RS("City") & vbTab & _
                    RS("State") & vbTab & _
                    RS("Zip")
  RS.MoveNext
Wend
RS.Close

'Dereference the Recordset
Set RS = Nothing

cmdDeleteRows.Enabled = True

End Sub
```

If your code executed correctly, your Grid should look something like the one you see in Figure 3-9.

Figure 3-9. A Grid displaying the remaining rows after a DELETE query

To further explore the many ways you can use the DELETE statement, try using different operators after the WHERE clause and desired column. Now change your code to execute the DELETE statement against the Contacts table without the WHERE clause in order to empty the table.

Summary

This chapter wraps up an exhaustive and example-filled look at what you can do with the DML statements allowed by ADOCE. So far, you've made minimal use of the Recordset object in order to execute both DDL and DML statements. In the next couple of chapters, you'll dive deep into the ADOCE Connection and Recordset objects to see how they can enhance your Pocket PC database applications.

CHAPTER 4

The ADOCE
Connection Object

AFTER TWO CHAPTERS WORTH of connecting to local Pocket Access databases and executing DDL and DML statements using the Recordset object, you're probably wondering what you need a Connection object for. You might be surprised to find out that you were using the Connection object all along. Every time you executed a DDL statement or a SQL query with the Recordset object, you also passed along a reference to the Pocket Access database you wanted to communicate with. Due to ADOCE's flat object model, you were able to use the Connection object implicitly to create a connection each time you used the Recordset object. This is fine when I'm trying to teach you Pocket SQL DDL or DML, but there are good reasons not to operate this way when you're building a production application.

The most time-consuming thing you can do is make a connection to a data source. Because you don't have the luxury of connection pooling on the Pocket PC, and you don't have any multiuser scalability issues when communicating with Pocket Access, you should look at creating a single connection to the database. Connecting to your Pocket Access database at the earliest appropriate time and releasing that connection once your application no longer needs any database services is the best way to increase the performance of your eMbedded Visual Basic database applications.

I know, you're probably freaking out right about now because this sounds like the single tier, monolithic, fat client applications you used to build back in the early '90s. Well, you're right, it is. But remember, only one person at a time is going to use your Pocket PC database application. You don't even have the option of putting your business logic in middle-tier COM+ objects. You're probably even having Visual Basic 3.0 flashbacks because you're having to put your business logic in Bas modules instead of classes or separate DLLs. Hopefully you'll feel nostalgic about all this instead of thinking that your programming skills are taking a big step backward in time.

There's another good reason to maintain a constant connection to the database throughout the life of your application: memory leaks. ADOCE has a well-known bug that causes it to leak memory every time it's closed and dereferenced. Years of making your Active Server Pages and 3-Tier Client/Server applications more scalable by closing and setting your objects to Nothing as soon as humanly possible now creates a big memory leak on your Pocket PC. This leak is big enough to eat through your 32MB of RAM (or 64MB if you have the new iPAQ). So forget about creating and connecting late and releasing and disconnecting early, and instead go ahead and use a global variable to maintain an open connection to your database.

 NOTE *Just in case you're wondering why I haven't brought up connecting to remote databases like SQL Server or Oracle, it's because the drivers either don't exist or aren't ready for prime time. What's frustrating is that the online help for ADOCE alludes to connecting to SQL Server using the SQLOLEDB Provider. The problem lies in the fact that when you try to make such a connection, an error is raised telling you that ADO cannot find the specified Provider. The Provider that comes with SQL Server CE 1.1/ADOCE 3.1 won't help you in this department either. It enables you to connect to your local SQL Server database, but it won't let you reach out across the network to connect to a remote one. So for now, we'll have to pass on building 2-Tier Client/Server applications on our Pocket PCs using the current ADOCE technology. A direct connection from a Pocket PC to a remote SQL database wouldn't work too well anyway due to the inherent unreliability of wireless networks.*

Just like in Chapter 3, you're going to need a test project in order to perform all the Connection examples in this chapter. Open up eMbedded Visual Basic and create a new project called "Connection." Because you're working with a database, set a reference to ADOCE.

Making the Connection

The only way to connect to a database using the Connection object is to use the Open method. That said, you do have some flexibility in the way you open a connection thanks to a few of the Connection object properties.

Syntax

Connection.Open([*ConnectionString* as String], [*UserID* as String], [*Password* as String])

Parameters

ConnectionString

This is an optional string used to open a data source. This string may contain the entire connection string or just the name of the data source.

UserID

This is an optional string used to pass the user's identifier to connect to the data source. This string is ignored if the user's identifier data is contained in the ConnectionString.

Password

This is an optional string used to pass the user's password to the data source. This string is ignored if the user's password data is contained in the ConnectionString.

Return Values

None.

Example

In this example, you'll connect to the DML database you created in Chapter 3 using the Open method of the Connection object. You'll also jump ahead of yourself and disconnect from the database using the Close method at the end. Drag a CommandButton from the Toolbox and drop it on your form. Name the CommandButton "cmdOpen" and set the caption to read "Open." In the click event of this CommandButton you'll insert code to both open and close the DML database.

```
Private Sub cmdOpen_Click()

    cmdOpen.Enabled = False

    'Declare variables
    Dim CN As ADOCE.Connection
    Set CN = CreateObject("ADOCE.Connection.3.0")
```

```
            'Open database
            CN.Open "\My Documents\DML.cdb"

            'Close the Connection
            CN.Close

            'Dereference the Connection
            Set CN = Nothing

            cmdOpen.Enabled = True

        End Sub
```

As you can see, you don't have to create a complicated ConnectionString as a parameter to the Open method. Because you're talking to Pocket Access, you just point to it. As you can also see, there's no security when it comes to Pocket Access databases as you didn't have to provide a UserID or Password. If you were going to connect to a remote SQL Server 7.0 database, given that you had the proper OLEDB Provider, the Open ConnectionString would look something like this:

```
CN.Open "Provider=SQLOLEDB;Data Source=Server1;Initial Catalog=pubs;User
Id=sa;Password=;"
```

If you choose to buy a copy of SQL Server 2000 in order to get your hands on SQL Server CE 1.1, your ConnectionString will look something similar to what's displayed in the preceding code line, with a slightly different Provider. A discussion of SQL Server CE is outside the scope of this book (indeed, it warrants a book of its own), so let's move along with our discussion of what's possible with Pocket Access.

Connection State

In the example showing you how to open a database, you didn't necessarily know if your code worked or not, other than the fact that your code didn't raise any errors. The easiest way to know if your database is open or closed at any given moment is to use the State property of the Connection object.

Syntax

Connection.State

Parameters

None.

Return Values

This property returns an Integer value. If the database is closed, this property returns a 0, which refers to the adStateClosed constant. If the database is open, this property returns a 1, which refers to the adStateOpen constant.

Example

This example uses the State property of the Connection object to enable you to toggle between being connected and disconnected from your DML database. At this point, I'll start putting the idea of a permanent connection to use. The first thing I want you to do is to add a Module to your Connection eMbedded Visual Basic project. You can just call it "Module1." Now drag a CommandButton from the Toolbox and drop it on your form. Name the CommandButton "cmdState" and set the caption to read "State." For your first bit of code, you'll need to jump over to your new module. In the General Declarations section of Module1, add the following line of code:

```
Dim CN As ADOCE.Connection
```

Now you have a global Connection variable declared that you can use throughout the life of this application. The next thing you need to do is add code to the Form's Load event to instantiate the Connection object and to set the caption of your State CommandButton to reflect the fact that the database is not yet open.

```
Private Sub Form_Load()

    'Instantiate the Connection Object
    Set CN = CreateObject("ADOCE.Connection.3.0")

    'Set State button's caption to closed
    cmdState.Caption = "State - Closed"


End Sub
```

Because you're using a global Connection variable, it's important to make sure that the Connection gets closed and dereferenced before your application closes. Normally, you'd put that kind of cleanup code in the Unload event of the main Visual Basic form. Unfortunately, things work a little differently in eMbedded Visual Basic. As you probably know by now, Pocket PC applications are closed by clicking the OK button in the top-right corner of the screen. Clicking that button triggers the Form's OKClick event. The App.End method is inserted in this event procedure by default to shut down the application. The unfortunate side effect of the End method is that it prevents the QueryUnload and the Unload event procedures from firing. Therefore, you need to perform your cleanup code in the OKClick event.

```
Private Sub Form_OKClick()

    If CN.State = 1 Then 'Open
            'Let's close the database
            CN.Close
    End If

    'Dereference the Connection
    Set CN = Nothing

    App.End

End Sub
```

If the connection is still open, it closes. The Connection object is dereferenced and then the App object's End method is called to shut down the program. For your last bit of code, in the click event of the cmdState CommandButton, insert the code that enables you to toggle your connection state.

```
Private Sub cmdState_Click()

    cmdState.Enabled = False

    If CN.State = 0 Then 'Closed

            'Let's open the database
            CN.Open "\My Documents\DML.cdb"
            'Set caption to Open
            cmdState.Caption = "State - Open"

    Else 'Open
```

```
          'Let's close the database
          CN.Close
          'Set caption to Closed
          cmdState.Caption = "State - Closed"
     End If

     cmdState.Enabled = True

End Sub
```

This code checks the state of the connection. It then opens a connection if the connection is closed or closes a connection if the connection is open. Additionally, it changes the CommandButton caption to accurately reflect the current connection state. If your code is working properly, your application should look something like Figure 4-1.

Figure 4-1. Toggling connection state

Provider

The Provider property sets or returns the OLE DB data provider for the given connection. Normally, I set the Provider in the ConnectionString parameter of the Connection object's Open method. On the other hand, setting the Provider before opening a connection aids in debugging. When the connection is closed, the Provider property is in read/write mode. Once a connection has been opened, this property is read-only until the connection is closed again. The Provider for a Pocket Access database is CEDB.

Syntax

Connection.Provider

Parameters

None.

Return Values

This property returns a string value.

Example

This example couldn't be simpler. Drag a CommandButton from the Toolbox and drop it on your form. Name the CommandButton "cmdProvider" and set the caption to read "Provider." In the click event of this CommandButton, insert the following line of code:

```
Private Sub cmdProvider_Click()

    CN.Provider = "CEDB"

End Sub
```

You should test out this code by toggling the State button back and forth between an open and closed connection. If your connection is closed, clicking the Provider button is pretty uneventful. On the other hand, if the connection is open, an error should be raised, as shown in Figure 4-2.

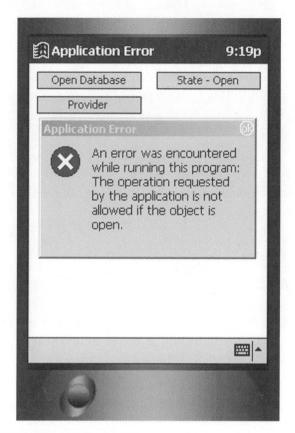

Figure 4-2. A Provider Application Error message

ConnectionString

The ConnectionString property contains the string used to connect to a data source. In the case of Pocket Access, this is the path to the database file. The Provider property should be set in advance of setting the ConnectionString.

```
CN.Provider = "CEDB"
CN.ConnectionString = "\My Documents\DML.cdb"
```

Just as with the Provider property, the ConnectionString property is in read/write mode when the connection is closed and is read-only when the connection is open.

Syntax

Connection.ConnectionString

Parameters

None.

Return Values

This property returns a string value.

Example

In this example, I'll show you how returning the current ConnectionString and displaying it in a MessageBox can be a valuable debugging tool. Drag a CommandButton from the Toolbox and drop it on your form. Name the CommandButton "cmdConnectionString" and set the caption to read "Connection String." Like before, toggle the State button before clicking the ConnectionString button.

```
Private Sub cmdConnectionString_Click()

        MsgBox CN.ConnectionString

End Sub
```

When the connection is closed, clicking the ConnectionString button doesn't return anything. When the connection is open, clicking the ConnectionString button displays the Provider and the path to your Pocket Access database, as shown in Figure 4-3.

Figure 4-3. Provider and ConnectionString information

Mode

The Mode property describes the permissions for modifying data for the current connection. Returning eight different types of read/write permission scenarios about a connection to a particular database, the Mode property may or may not provide a wealth of information depending on the type of database you're connected to. The Mode property always returns a value of 3, denoting (read/write) permissions for Pocket Access databases.

Syntax

Connection.Mode

Parameters

None.

Return Values

The Mode property returns one of the Integer values listed in Table 4-1.

Table 4-1. The Mode Constants Table

CONSTANT	VALUE	DESCRIPTION
adModeUnknown	0	Permissions have not yet been set
adModeRead	1	Read-only permissions
adModeWrite	2	Write-only permissions
adModeReadWrite	3	Read/write permissions
adModeShareDenyRead	4	Prevents others from opening a connection with read permissions
adModeShareDenyWrite	8	Prevents others from opening a connection with write permissions
adModeShareExclusive	12	Prevents others from opening a connection
adModeShareDenyNone	16	Allows others to open a connection with any permissions, and restricts others from denying read/write access to anyone

Example

This example displays the Mode for your DML Pocket Access database.
Drag a CommandButton from the Toolbox and drop it on your form. Name the
CommandButton "cmdMode" and set the caption to read "Mode."

```
Private Sub cmdMode_Click()

        MsgBox CN.Mode

End Sub
```

The code should have returned a value of 3, conveying that you have
read/write access to the DML Pocket Access database, as shown in Figure 4-4.

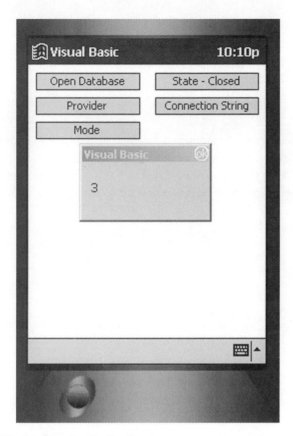

Figure 4-4. The Mode value for Pocket Access

Errors

The Errors property returns a Collection of errors from the OLE DB Provider. You iterate through the Errors Collection using the For—Each—Next statements. It's important to check the Errors property every time you open a connection because so many things can go wrong. It's particularly important because the On Error Resume Next statement would normally suppress these possible connection errors.

Syntax

Connection.Errors

Parameters

None.

Return Values

This property returns a Collection of Error objects.

Example

In this example you're going to attempt to use the SQLOLEDB Provider alluded to in the ADOCE help files in order to connect to a remote SQL Server. Because you've included the On Error Resume Next statement, you'll have to rely on the Connection Errors Collection to tell you if anything went wrong.

```
Private Sub cmdErrors_Click()

        On Error Resume Next

        'Declare variables
        Dim CN As ADOCE.Connection
        Dim e As Variant
        Set CN = CreateObject("ADOCE.Connection.3.0")

        'Connect to a remote SQL Server 2000 box
        CN.ConnectionString = "Provider=SQLOLEDB;Data Source=Trident2;Initial
        Catalog=pubs;User Id=sa;Password=;"
        CN.Open CN.ConnectionString

        'Display errors
        For Each e In CN.Errors
                MsgBox e.Description
        Next

        CN.Close

        'Dereference the Connection
        Set CN = Nothing

End Sub
```

Iterating through the Errors Collection should have turned up the error shown in Figure 4-5.

Figure 4-5. The error message when ADO cannot find the specified Provider

Transactions

When you withdraw money from an ATM machine, several things happen behind the scenes in order to get you the cash you requested. Once your identification is validated, the ATM allows you to deposit money, withdraw money, check account balances, and move money between your accounts, among other things. While it may seem that these things happen quickly and easily, many complex operations are occurring to make sure that your money gets to the right place without getting lost. Dollar bills aren't flying around between ATMs and bank accounts.

What's really happening is that the databases that maintain tables with your account balances are being updated using SQL. When you take $10.00 out of your checking account, an UPDATE query is executed to subtract the money from your account balance. Likewise, when you move that $10.00 to your savings account, an UPDATE query is executed to add the money to your account balance. What do you think would happen if the ATM system suddenly lost power or connectivity between the time that your checking account is debited and your savings account is credited? If it weren't for transactions, your $10.00 would go into never-never land. Transactions allow two or more database actions to act as one. In other words, if the updates to both your checking and savings accounts don't succeed together, neither of them is committed in their respective databases and is rolled back. The action of rolling back a transaction returns the databases to their original state so that your $10.00 stays in the checking account.

The ADOCE Connection object provides you with three methods to let you use transactions in your own database applications. The BeginTrans method starts a new transaction for a given connection. The CommitTrans method commits the current transaction for the given connection. The RollbackTrans method cancels any changes made during the current transaction and ends the transaction for the given connection. These three methods are all you need to ensure that your business-critical operations either all succeed together or are returned to their original states. These methods can be used if your OLE DB Provider supports them. Based on what you've seen of Pocket SQL so far, it probably won't surprise you to know that they don't work on Pocket Access databases. Nevertheless, it's important to understand transactions, as you may find yourself working with SQL Server CE at some point in the future.

Fictitious Transaction Example

You will be able to execute transactions against databases that have OLE DB Providers, such as SQL Server CE 1.1. For now, I'll show you what the code for performing transactions should look like. In some places, comments will take the place of the SQL used to perform updates in order to illustrate the flow properly. Drag a CommandButton from the Toolbox and drop it on your form. Name the CommandButton "cmdTransactions" and set the caption to read "Transactions." In the click event, insert the following code:

```
Private Sub cmdTransactions_Click()

        On Error Resume Next

        'Declare Error variable
        Dim e As Variant

        'Start the transaction
        CN.BeginTrans

                'Run an UPDATE query to
                'debit the checking account
```

```
                'Check for errors
                For Each e In CN.Errors
                        If e.Number <> 0 Then

                                'Display the error
                                MsgBox e.Description
                                'An error occurred
                                CN.RollbackTrans
                                'Exit the subroutine
                                Exit Sub

                        End If
                Next

        'Run an UPDATE query to
        'credit the savings account

        'Check for errors
        For Each e In CN.Errors
                If e.Number <> 0 Then

                                'Display the error
                                MsgBox e.Description
                                'An error occurred
                                CN.RollbackTrans
                                'Exit the subroutine
                                Exit Sub

                End If
        Next

        'You made it!
        CN.CommitTrans

End Sub
```

If you toggle the State button to open a connection, you can click the
Transactions button and see an error displayed as a result of your error-handling
code. The error you caught will tell you that these three transactional methods
aren't supported by Pocket Access, as displayed in Figure 4-6.

Figure 4-6. The OLE DB Provider doesn't support transactions

Execute

The Execute method executes a command against the given connection. Basically, you can use the Execute method of the Connection object to perform almost any kind of DDL or DML operation. Yes, all those operations you performed in previous chapters using the Recordset object could have been done using the Connection object. Remember, the Recordset object is always creating a connection in the background. Because ADOCE doesn't provide a Command object like its ADO 2.6 big brother, you can execute stored procedures using the Connection object as well. Unfortunately, you can't connect directly to a database that supports stored procedures at the moment.

Syntax

When the command does not return rows (like an UPDATE):
Connection.Execute(CommandText as String, [RecordsAffected as Long])
    When the command does return rows (like a SELECT):
Recordset = Connection.Execute(CommandText as String, [RecordsAffected as Long])

Parameters

CommandText

This is the command to execute against the given connection. The syntax of the string to be used for this parameter is Provider-specific. The string can be standard SQL syntax or any type of command that the Provider supports.

RecordsAffected

This is an optional variable for obtaining the number of affected records.

Return Values

This method returns a Recordset if the CommandText command is able to generate one.

Example

This example provides a good segue into the next chapter on Recordsets by executing a SELECT statement that returns rows that you can loop through. Drag a CommandButton from the Toolbox and drop it on your form. Name the CommandButton "cmdExecute" and set the caption to read "Execute." In the click event, insert the following code:

```
Private Sub cmdExecute_Click()

    Dim RS As ADOCE.Recordset

    'Calling the Execute Method with
    'a SQL query that returns rows
    'causes the Execute Method to
    'return a Recordset
```

```
        Set RS = CN.Execute("SELECT * FROM Contacts")

        'Loop through the results
        While Not RS.EOF

                'Display the ContactID, First Name,
                'and Last Name in a MessageBox
                MsgBox RS(0) & " " & RS(1) & " " & RS(2)
                RS.MoveNext
        Wend

        'Close the Recordset
        RS.Close

        'Dereference the Recordset object
        Set RS = Nothing

End Sub
```

Keep in mind that when you return a Recordset using the Execute method, you don't have all the options and fine control over the type of Recordset you want to return. If your code executed properly, it should display a MessageBox with Recordset data (see Figure 4-7).

Figure 4-7. A Recordset has been returned

Summary

I've now covered all the important methods and properties of the Connection object that you need to get connected and then some. You've learned how to increase your applications' performance by maintaining a constant connection to your Pocket Access database, and you found out that there seems to be some overlap between what the Connection object can do and what you can accomplish with the Recordset object. With that said, let's go see what makes the Recordset object so special.

CHAPTER 5

The ADOCE
Recordset Object

WE'VE FINALLY MADE it to the final building block needed to create database applications on the Pocket PC. SQL DML enables you to build databases and the Connection object enables you to connect to databases, but the Recordset object is definitely where the action is. When you execute a query that returns rows of data, ADOCE packages those rows together in a Recordset object. This Recordset object presents itself to you in the form of a virtual table with a subset of columns and rows that match up with the actual columns and rows found in the database table you're running a query against. Unfortunately, the ADOCE Recordset object lacks many of the features provided by its desktop and server cousins. You won't be able to use things like data shaping and disconnected Recordsets, and you won't have the ability to search within the Recordset and save your records as XML. Don't panic! You'll find a way to get along without all those cool features.

 NOTE *Even though you can do just about anything with the Recordset object, its use comes with a slight performance penalty due to object instantiation and the overhead of filling a virtual table. Therefore, I recommend that you only use it for obvious things like retrieving data.*

Yet again, you're going to need a test project in order to perform all the Recordset examples in this chapter. Open up eMbedded Visual Basic and create a new project called "Recordset." Add a module to your project called "Module1" and set a reference to ADOCE. You now need to add what I'll call "standard connection code" in all the right places just like you did in Chapter 4. Just in case you forgot, add the following line of code to the General Declarations section of Module1:

```
Public CN As ADOCE.Connection
```

Now add code to the Form's Load event to instantiate the Connection object and open the database. Don't forget to add proper error-handling code to check for connection errors.

```
Private Sub Form_Load()

        On Error Resume Next

        Dim e As Variant

        'Instantiate the Connection Object
        Set CN = CreateObject("ADOCE.Connection.3.0")

        'Open the database
        CN.Open "\My Documents\DML.cdb"

        'Display Connection Errors
        For Each e In CN.Errors
                MsgBox e.Description
        Next

End Sub
```

To make sure that the Connection gets closed and dereferenced before your application closes, add Connection object cleanup code in the OKClick event.

```
Private Sub Form_OKClick()

        If CN.State = 1 Then 'Open
                'Let's close the database
                CN.Close
        End If

        'Dereference the Connection
        Set CN = Nothing

        App.End

End Sub
```

Remember to use this boilerplate standard connection code in your future database projects and in the examples throughout the rest of this book.

Opening a Recordset

A lot of things go into opening a Recordset object. You have to determine what kind of cursor to use, what kind of locking to use, and what kind of query to run, to name a few. How you decide to set the various Recordset properties plays a big role in what you're allowed to do with the data.

Source

The Source property is where you define the source of the data you're looking for. This can typically be a SQL string or the name of a table.

```
'A SQL Query
rs.Source = "SELECT * FROM Contacts"
```

Or

```
'A Table
"Contacts"
```

The previous Source examples display the possible strings you can use in the context of your DML database and Contacts table.

ActiveConnection

The ActiveConnection property gives you the ability to set the current database connection for use by the Recordset. This can be a variable containing an open Connection object.

```
'An Object Variable
rs.ActiveConnection = CN
```

This can also be a valid connection string.

```
'A Path to the Database File
rs.ActiveConnection = "\My Documents\DML.cdb"
```

CursorType

The CursorType property identifies what kind of cursor you're using in order to let you know how you can move through the Recordset and how changes to the actual database are reflected in your Recordset. The four different kinds of cursors allowed by ADOCE are displayed in Table 5-1.

Table 5-1. ADOCE Cursors

CURSORTYPE	VALUE	DESCRIPTION
adOpenForwardOnly	0	This uses a forward-only cursor. It provides you with a static copy of a set of records where additions, changes, or deletions by other users are not visible. Use of this cursor does not improve performance.
adOpenKeyset	1	This uses a keyset-driven cursor. Additions and deletions by other users are not visible but data changes are. All types of movement through the Recordset are enabled.
adOpenDynamic	2	This uses a dynamic cursor. Additions, changes, and deletions by other users are visible, and all types of movement through the Recordset are allowed. Bookmarks may be used only if the provider supports them.
adOpenStatic	3	This uses a static cursor. It provides you with a static copy of a set of records where additions, changes, or deletions by other users are not visible. All types of movement are possible.

NOTE *You should know that Pocket Access does not support dynamic and static cursors.*

LockType

The LockType property sets or returns the kind of database lock being used when opening a Recordset. The three different kinds of locks supported by ADOCE are displayed in Table 5-2.

Table 5-2. ADOCE Locks

LOCKTYPE	VALUE	DESCRIPTION
adLockReadOnly	1	Read-only locking. You cannot add, delete, or change records.
adLockPessimistic	2	Pessimistic locking, record by record. To ensure the successful editing of the records, the provider usually locks records at the data source immediately upon editing. You can add, delete, and change records.
adLockOptimistic	3	Optimistic locking, record by record. The provider uses optimistic locking, locking records only when you call the Recordset object's Update method. You can add, delete, and change records.

NOTE *Pocket Access does not support pessimistic locking.*

Options

The options specify how the OLE DB Provider should evaluate the Source property, as shown in Table 5-3.

Table 5-3. ADOCE Options

OPTION	VALUE	DESCRIPTION
adCmdText	1	Evaluates the Source property as a SQL statement.
adCmdTable	2	Evaluates the Source property as a table name from the system table MSysTables.
adCmdStoredProc	4	Evaluates the Source property as a stored procedure from the system table MSysProcs.
adCmdUnknown	8	Evaluates the Source property as unknown.
adCmdTableDirect	512	Evaluates the Source property as a table name whose columns are all returned.

NOTE *The four previously described properties, including Source, ActiveConnection, CursorType, and LockType, are most commonly used as parameters to the Recordset object's Open method.*

Open and Close

Now that I've discussed all the properties that affect how a Recordset behaves when it's opened, let's put these pieces together. When you use these properties as parameters of the Open method, the syntax is as follows:

Recordset.Open Source, [ActiveConnection], [CursorType], [LockType], [Options]

Even though it's optional, you should always include your Connection object variable in the ActiveConnection parameter. If you decide only to include the Source and ActiveConnection parameters when calling the Open method, the Recordset will behave in its default mode, which gives you a forward-only cursor and a read-only lock.

```
'Declare variables
Dim RS As ADOCE.Recordset
Set RS = CreateObject("ADOCE.Recordset.3.0")

'The default, forward-only, read-only Recordset
```

```
RS.Open "SELECT * FROM Contacts", CN

'Close and dereference the Recordset
RS.Close
Set RS = Nothing
```

This same forward-only, read-only Recordset with all the optional parameters included would have an Open method that looks like this:

```
RS.Open "SELECT * FROM Contacts", CN, adOpenForwardOnly, adLockReadOnly, adCmdText
```

This is fine for most instances when you want to return a snapshot of data that you have no intention of manipulating. Remember, unlike ADO 2.6 on the server and desktop, you don't get a big fire hose performance boost by using a forward-only cursor. This begs the question, "Why use it?" Dynamic and static cursors aren't available to you, but the keyset cursor is and that gives you the flexibility to write to the database and scroll back and forth through the Recordset.

```
'Declare variables
Dim RS As ADOCE.Recordset
Set RS = CreateObject("ADOCE.Recordset.3.0")

'A keyset-based, forward and backward, read and write Recordset
RS.Open "SELECT * FROM Contacts", CN, adOpenKeyset, adLockOptimistic, adCmdText

'Close and dereference the Recordset
RS.Close
Set RS = Nothing
```

So far, you've used the two cursors and two locks that are available to you when working with Pocket Access. You've also included the option adCmdText to specify that your Source argument is a SQL statement. The only possible combinations of Open method parameters left are those that open an entire table directly or that call stored procedures. There are two reasons to open a table directly: if you would've used SELECT * against the table in question or if you need to add, update, or delete data in that table. Let's take a look at how to open a table without using SQL.

```
'Declare variables
Dim RS As ADOCE.Recordset
Set RS = CreateObject("ADOCE.Recordset.3.0")

'A keyset-based, forward and backward, read and write Recordset against a table
```

```
RS.Open "Contacts", CN, adOpenKeyset, adLockOptimistic, adCmdTable

'Close and dereference the Recordset
RS.Close
Set RS = Nothing
```

You are now left with stored procedures as the last things you can open with your combination of parameters. You can't call remote SQL Servers that support stored procedures, and for some reason even the local version of SQL Server CE doesn't support stored procedures. Surely, Pocket Access doesn't support this high-end feature. Believe it or not, there is a system table called MSysProcs that stores SQL statements in a stored procedure–like fashion. I'm going to call them "wannabe" stored procedures and I'm not going to spend any time on them because they lack two things that make true stored procedures worth having: They don't give you a performance boost over dynamic SQL and they don't accept parameters. Furthermore, you don't even call them using the adCmdStoredProc option—go figure.

Traversing the Recordset

Well, if you thought that opening and closing Recordsets was fun, now you get to loop through them and display their data. Once you've opened a Recordset, your cursor is placed on the first record.

Moving between BOF and EOF

The bookends that mark the upper and lower bounds of a Recordset are known as the End of File (EOF) and Beginning of File (BOF). Between these two places are the actual records that make up the Recordset. These two properties return True or False depending on your cursor location. If the current record position is before the first record, BOF returns True. Likewise, if the record position is after the last record, EOF returns True. If both BOF and EOF return True, you have an empty Recordset.

```
If RS.BOF And RS.EOF Then
        MsgBox "You have an empty Recordset"
End If
```

EOF is the most frequently used of the pair. It is usually combined with one of eMbedded Visual Basic's looping statements to mark the end of the loop.

```
While Not RS.EOF
        'Do Something
      RS.MoveNext
Wend
```

   Or

```
Do While Not RS.EOF
        'Do Something
      RS.MoveNext
Loop
```

   Or
```
Do Until RS.EOF
    'Do Something
    RS.MoveNext
Loop
```

MoveNext

As you can see, the MoveNext method is also used with the loops. MoveNext is integral if you want to make it to EOF. Each time the loop goes around, the MoveNext method moves the cursor ahead one record until you reach the end. To better illustrate this, add the Grid control to your project by dragging it from the Toolbox and dropping it onto the form like you did back in Chapter 3. Just like before, make sure to set the Cols property equal to 8 and the Rows property equal to 0. Now drag a CommandButton from the Toolbox and drop it on your form. Name this control "cmdForwardOnly" and set its caption to read "Forward Only." In the click event of this CommandButton, insert the following code:

```
Private Sub cmdForwardOnly_Click()

        'Declare variables
        Dim RS As ADOCE.Recordset
        Dim i As Integer
        Set RS = CreateObject("ADOCE.Recordset.3.0")
```

```
'A forward-only, read-only Recordset
RS.Open "Contacts", CN, adOpenForwardOnly, adLockReadOnly, adCmdTable

'Remove existing data from Grid
For i = 1 To GridCtrl1.Rows
        GridCtrl1.RemoveItem 0
Next

While Not RS.EOF
        GridCtrl1.AddItem RS("ContactID") & vbTab & _
                          RS("FirstName") & vbTab & _
                          RS("LastName") & vbTab & _
                          RS("CompanyName") & vbTab & _
                          RS("StreetAddress") & vbTab & _
                          RS("City") & vbTab & _
                          RS("State") & vbTab & _
                          RS("Zip")
        RS.MoveNext
Wend

'Close and dereference the Recordset
RS.Close
Set RS = Nothing

End Sub
```

TIP *Remember, if you are using CE 2.x, the Recordset declaration should leave off the version number.*

If your code executed correctly, your Grid should look something like the one you see in Figure 5-1.

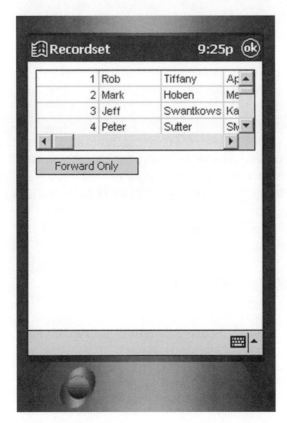

Figure 5-1. The Grid displaying the results of moving to EOF

MoveFirst, MoveLast, and MovePrevious

You've seen how the MoveNext method works, but what about MoveFirst, MovePrevious, and MoveLast? As their names suggest, calling them either moves the current record position to the first record, the last record, or the previous record in the Recordset. Let's build an example to make the use of these methods clear. The first thing you need to do is put a global Recordset object into place in the same way you did with the Connection object. In the General Declarations section of Module1, insert the following line of code underneath the global Connection object declaration:

```
Public RS As ADOCE.Recordset
```

The next thing you need to do is instantiate the Recordset object and open the Recordset in the Load event of your Form underneath all the Connection object loading code:

```
'Instantiate the Recordset Object
Set RS = CreateObject("ADOCE.Recordset.3.0")

'A keyset-based, forward and backward, read and write Recordset
RS.Open "Contacts", CN, adOpenKeyset, adLockOptimistic, adCmdTable
```

With these global Recordset object pieces in place, you can now start implementing the code needed to move the cursor around and display the contents of the current record in the Grid control. To implement the MoveFirst code, drag a CommandButton from the Toolbox and drop it on your form. Name this control "cmdMoveFirst" and set its caption to read "Move First." In the click event of this CommandButton, insert the following code:

```
Private Sub cmdMoveFirst_Click()

        Dim i As Integer

        RS.MoveFirst

        'Remove existing data from Grid
        For i = 1 To GridCtrl1.Rows
                GridCtrl1.RemoveItem 0
        Next

        GridCtrl1.AddItem RS("ContactID") & vbTab & _
                        RS("FirstName") & vbTab & _
                        RS("LastName") & vbTab & _
                        RS("CompanyName") & vbTab & _
                        RS("StreetAddress") & vbTab & _
                        RS("City") & vbTab & _
                        RS("State") & vbTab & _
                        RS("Zip")

End Sub
```

To implement the MoveLast code, drag a CommandButton from the Toolbox and drop it on your form. Name this control "cmdMoveLast" and set its caption to read "Move Last." In the click event of this CommandButton, insert the following code:

```
Private Sub cmdMoveLast_Click()

        Dim i As Integer
```

```
        RS.MoveLast

        'Remove existing data from Grid
        For i = 1 To GridCtrl1.Rows
                GridCtrl1.RemoveItem 0
        Next

        GridCtrl1.AddItem RS("ContactID") & vbTab & _
                        RS("FirstName") & vbTab & _
                        RS("LastName") & vbTab & _
                        RS("CompanyName") & vbTab & _
                        RS("StreetAddress") & vbTab & _
                        RS("City") & vbTab & _
                        RS("State") & vbTab & _
                        RS("Zip")


End Sub
```

To implement the MoveNext code, drag a CommandButton from the Toolbox and drop it on your form. Name this control "cmdMoveNext" and set its caption to read "Move Next." In the click event of this CommandButton, go ahead and insert the following code:

```
Private Sub cmdMoveNext_Click()

        Dim i As Integer

        RS.MoveNext

        'Remove existing data from Grid
        For i = 1 To GridCtrl1.Rows
                GridCtrl1.RemoveItem 0
        Next

        GridCtrl1.AddItem RS("ContactID") & vbTab & _
                        RS("FirstName") & vbTab & _
                        RS("LastName") & vbTab & _
                        RS("CompanyName") & vbTab & _
                        RS("StreetAddress") & vbTab & _
                        RS("City") & vbTab & _
                        RS("State") & vbTab & _
                        RS("Zip")


End Sub
```

To implement the MovePrevious code, drag a CommandButton from the Toolbox and drop it on your form. Name this control "cmdMovePrevious" and set its caption to read "Move Previous." In the click event of this CommandButton, insert the following code:

```
Private Sub cmdMovePrevious_Click()

        Dim i As Integer

        RS.MovePrevious

        'Remove existing data from Grid
        For i = 1 To GridCtrl1.Rows
                GridCtrl1.RemoveItem 0
        Next

        GridCtrl1.AddItem RS("ContactID") & vbTab & _
                        RS("FirstName") & vbTab & _
                        RS("LastName") & vbTab & _
                        RS("CompanyName") & vbTab & _
                        RS("StreetAddress") & vbTab & _
                        RS("City") & vbTab & _
                        RS("State") & vbTab & _
                        RS("Zip")

End Sub
```

Now that you have all the necessary code in place to traverse the Recordset in either direction, go ahead and run the program, click the various cursor-moving buttons, and view the changes in the Grid, as shown in Figure 5-2.

Figure 5-2. The Grid displaying the current record

Because you didn't include any error handling or measures to prevent going past the first or last record, the execution of your MoveFirst and MovePrevious methods will eventually lead to an error that looks like the one in Figure 5-3.

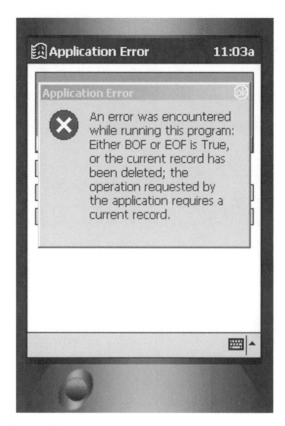

Figure 5-3. A BOF or EOF error

Bookmark

Sometimes when you're moving through a Recordset, you find a record of interest that you'd like to be able to return to easily. The Recordset object provides a property called Bookmark to do just that. There are a few requirements that you have to meet in order to be able to save your place in a Recordset.

- The OLE DB Provider you're using must support Bookmarks, which Pocket Access does.

- You must use a cursor that supports going forward and backward through a Recordset.

- A saved Bookmark only works as long as the Recordset is open.

- Two Recordsets cannot share a common Bookmark.

Now that you know the requirements for using a Bookmark, let's build an example. You'll need a global Variant variable for the Bookmark as well as a global Boolean variable to reflect whether or not a Bookmark has been set. In the General Declarations section of Module1, insert the following lines of code underneath the global Recordset object declaration:

```
Public MyBookMark As Variant
Public MyBookMarkSet As Boolean
```

In the Load event of the Form, add the following code to reflect the fact that the Bookmark has not yet been set:

```
'There are no bookmarks set yet
MyBookMarkSet = False
```

Now it's time to implement the code necessary to set the Bookmark equal to whatever record you happen to be looking at in the Grid. In order to prevent possible errors, check to make sure that the OLE DB Provider allows for the use of Bookmarks by using the Supports method of the Recordset object. Drag a CommandButton from the Toolbox and drop it on your form. Name this control "cmdSetBookmark" and set its caption to read "Set Bookmark." In the click event of this CommandButton, insert the following code:

```
Private Sub cmdSetBookmark_Click()

        If RS.Supports(adBookmark) Then
                'Set bookmark variable equal to the current record
                MyBookMark = RS.Bookmark
                'The bookmark is set
                MyBookMarkSet = True
        Else
                MsgBox "Bookmarks aren't supported"
        End If

End Sub
```

In the previous code, if the Bookmark property is supported, it's set to the current record and the Boolean MyBookMarkSet variable is set to True to let you know that the Bookmark is currently in use. With the Bookmark set, you now need to implement the code that will get you back to your bookmarked record once you've moved the cursor somewhere else in the Recordset. Drag a CommandButton from the Toolbox and drop it on your form. Name this control "cmdGotoBookmark" and set its caption to read "Go to Bookmark." In the click event of this CommandButton, insert the following code:

```
Private Sub cmdGotoBookmark_Click()

        If MyBookMarkSet = True Then

                'Move record pointer to the bookmarked record
                RS.Bookmark = MyBookMark

                Dim i As Integer

                'Remove existing data from Grid
                For i = 1 To GridCtrl1.Rows
                        GridCtrl1.RemoveItem 0
                Next

                        GridCtrl1.AddItem RS("ContactID") & vbTab & _
                                RS("FirstName") & vbTab & _
                                RS("LastName") & vbTab & _
                                RS("CompanyName") & vbTab & _
                                RS("StreetAddress") & vbTab & _
                                RS("City") & vbTab & _
                                RS("State") & vbTab & _
                                RS("Zip")
        Else
                MsgBox "There are no Bookmarks currently set"
        End If

End Sub
```

As you can see in the previous code, you first check to see if the Bookmark is actually set before executing the code. You then move the record pointer to the desired Bookmark and fill the Grid with that record's data. Now run the program and follow these steps to ensure that your code is working properly:

1. Click the Move First button to display the first record in the Grid.

2. Click the Move Next button to display the second record in the Grid.

3. Click the Set Bookmark button to save the second record for later retrieval.

4. Click the Move Last button to display the fourth record.

5. Click the Go to Bookmark button to return to your bookmarked record.

Were you taken back to the second record? If your code worked correctly, your application should look like Figure 5-4.

Figure 5-4. The Bookmarked record displayed in the Grid

The Fields Object and Collection

Even though you haven't seen the word "Fields" yet, it's fair to say that you've been working with them all along. Fields are the columns of a Recordset. If you'll remember back to Chapter 3, you used the Fields Collection and object to tell you the names and data types of columns in the tables that you were iterating through. I'm not going to rehash all the things presented in Chapter 3—I'll only cover a couple of things of interest.

Default Values

There are several ways to access the data in a Field. It can be accessed either by field name or by column number starting with zero.

```
RS.Fields("ContactID").Value
RS.Fields(0).Value
```

The Value property shown previously is the default property for the Fields Collection and can therefore be omitted with no difference in the outcome.

```
RS.Fields("ContactID")
RS.Fields(0)
```

You can take this omission one step further when you realize that the Fields Collection is the default Collection of the Recordset object.

```
RS("ContactID")
RS(0)
```

Talk about a savings in the typing of code. As you have probably already noticed, all my code examples have used the last method of displaying fields. Live it up while you can because this shorthand type of coding goes away when programming against the .NET Framework.

Obtaining Metadata

I always instruct you to set the Cols property of the Grid control to 8. This is because I know in advance how many columns will be returned. What if you don't know how many columns will be returned from a table? What if you don't even know the column names? Using the Field Collection is really handy when you require the dynamic discovery of metadata from a table. Of course, why stop there when you can get the actual data along with the metadata dynamically without having to know anything about the table you're calling? To illustrate how to do this, drag a CommandButton from the Toolbox and drop it on your form. Name this control "cmdMetadata" and set its caption to read "Get Metadata." In the click event of this CommandButton, insert the following code:

```
Private Sub cmdMetadata_Click()

        'Declare variables
        Dim RS As ADOCE.Recordset
        Dim i As Integer
```

```
Dim ColumnNames As String
Dim ColumnValues As String
Set RS = CreateObject("ADOCE.Recordset.3.0")

'A keyset-based, forward and backward, read and write Recordset
RS.Open "Contacts", CN, adOpenKeyset, adLockOptimistic, adCmdTable


'Remove existing data from Grid
For i = 1 To GridCtrl1.Rows
        GridCtrl1.RemoveItem 0
Next

'Set the Grid columns equal to the field count
GridCtrl1.Cols = RS.Fields.Count

'Get the column names
For i = 0 To RS.Fields.Count - 1
        ColumnNames = ColumnNames & RS.Fields(i).Name & vbTab
Next

'Add the column headers to the Grid
GridCtrl1.AddItem ColumnNames

'Loop through the Recordset
While Not RS.EOF

        'Get the column values for this row
        For i = 0 To RS.Fields.Count - 1
                ColumnValues = ColumnValues & RS.Fields(i).Value & vbTab
        Next

        'Add the column values to the row
        GridCtrl1.AddItem ColumnValues

        'Set ColumnValues to a zero-length string
        'so it can be refilled with the next row
        ColumnValues = ""

        RS.MoveNext
    Wend
```

```
            'Close and dereference the Recordset
            RS.Close
            Set RS = Nothing

    End Sub
```

As you can see from the previous code, the Fields Collection is the key to dynamic data and metadata retrieval. First of all, getting the Field count enables you to set the Grid to the proper number of columns. Next, iterating through the Fields Collection gives you the Column names in order to display the column headers in the Grid. Finally, iterating through the Fields Collection each time you loop through the Recordset gives you the column data for each row. This code will become very useful in Chapter 7 when you build a Pocket Access database manager.

Adding Data

When it comes to adding data to a table, there's more than one way to skin a cat. You've already learned how to add records through the INSERT statement. Now you will add the AddNew method of the Recordset object to your bag of tricks. This should be considered a mixed bag, of course. On the downside, using the AddNew method to insert records requires the overhead of instantiating the Recordset object, whereas executing the DML INSERT statement against the Connection object is much faster. On the upside, you get to use the EditMode property to tell you if someone else is editing the records you're about to add to. Of course, there's not much danger of that happening when you work with Pocket Access because you're not in a multiuser environment. The other benefit of inserting data with AddNew is that you can change your mind at the last second using the CancelUpdate method. For instance, in the unlikely event that someone else is performing an edit when you call the AddNew method, you would want to cancel your insert by calling the CancelUpdate method. On the other hand, if all goes well, you call the Update method, which commits the change to the database.

The best way to understand how AddNew, EditMode, Update, and CancelUpdate can all work together is to build an example. Drag a Command-Button from the Toolbox and drop it on your form. Name this control "cmdAdd" and set its caption to read "Add." In the click event of this CommandButton, insert the following code:

```
Private Sub cmdAdd_Click()

        'Declare variables
        Dim i As Integer
        Dim FirstName As String
        Dim LastName As String
        Dim CompanyName As String
        Dim StreetAddress As String
        Dim City As String
        Dim State As String
        Dim Zip As String
        Dim ColumnNames As String
        Dim ColumnValues As String

        'Get user input
        FirstName = InputBox("Enter a First Name", "AddNew")
        LastName = InputBox("Enter a Last Name", "AddNew")
        CompanyName = InputBox("Enter a Company Name", "AddNew")
        StreetAddress = InputBox("Enter a Street Address", "AddNew")
        City = InputBox("Enter a City", "AddNew")
        State = InputBox("Enter a State", "AddNew")
        Zip = InputBox("Enter a Zip Code", "AddNew")

        'Code to autoincrement the Primary Key
        Dim AutoNumber As Integer
        Dim Identity As ADOCE.Recordset
        Set Identity = CreateObject("ADOCE.Recordset.3.0")
        Identity.Open "SELECT ContactID FROM Contacts ORDER BY ContactID DESC", CN
        AutoNumber = CInt(Identity(0)) + 1
        Identity.Close

        'check to see if there's any editing in progress
        If RS.EditMode <> adEditNone Then
                MsgBox "There's editing in progress. Try the operation again later."
                Exit Sub
        End If

        'Add the new record
        RS.AddNew
        RS("ContactID") = AutoNumber
```

```
        RS("FirstName") = FirstName
        RS("LastName") = LastName
        RS("CompanyName") = CompanyName
        RS("StreetAddress") = StreetAddress
        RS("City") = City
        RS("State") = State
        RS("Zip") = Zip


        'Ask user if he or she wants the record added
        If MsgBox("Do you wish to add this record?", vbYesNoCancel) = vbYes Then
                RS.Update
        Else
                RS.CancelUpdate
                MsgBox "No new record added."
        End If


        'Query the database again to refresh the Grid
        RS.Requery


        'Remove existing data from Grid
        For i = 1 To GridCtrl1.Rows
                GridCtrl1.RemoveItem 0
        Next


        'Set the Grid columns equal to the field count
        GridCtrl1.Cols = RS.Fields.Count


        'Get the column names
        For i = 0 To RS.Fields.Count - 1
                ColumnNames = ColumnNames & RS.Fields(i).Name & vbTab
        Next


        'Add the column headers to the Grid
        GridCtrl1.AddItem ColumnNames


        'Loop through the Recordset
        While Not RS.EOF


                'Get the column values for this row
                For i = 0 To RS.Fields.Count - 1
                        ColumnValues = ColumnValues & RS.Fields(i).Value & vbTab
                Next


                'Add the column values to the row
```

```
GridCtrl1.AddItem ColumnValues

'Set ColumnValues to a zero-length string
'so it can be refilled with the next row
ColumnValues = ""

RS.MoveNext
Wend

End Sub
```

There's a lot of code back there, so let's walk through it and go over what's going on each step of the way. At the beginning, a bunch of InputBoxes are thrown up that ask the user to enter the data that's to be added, as you can see shown in Figure 5-5.

The next thing that happens after the data entry is complete is a separate Recordset is opened against the same table in order to find out the value of the

Figure 5-5. An InputBox asking for the user's first name

highest ContactID number. Remember the AutoNumber code you used earlier in the book to take care of Pocket Access' lack of an autoincrementing key field? Well, you need that code to make your AddNew work properly against your Contacts table. The next thing you do is use your new EditMode friend to tell you if anyone else is currently editing your record. If editing is in progress, you tell the user to try again later and then exit the subroutine. Because it's just you and your Pocket PC, I doubt there will be a problem here. Now that you have the data you need and a green light from the EditMode property, the AddNew method is called and all of the appropriate fields are set equal to the new data you entered. Just before the Update method is called, you throw up your "last chance to change your mind" MessageBox, as shown in Figure 5-6.

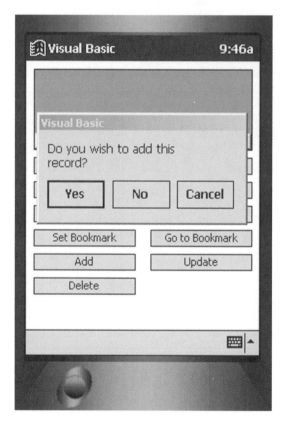

Figure 5-6. A Yes/No MessageBox prompting the user to add the record

If the user chooses Yes, the Update method is called and the new row of data is committed to the table. If, on the other hand, the user chooses No, the CancelUpdate method is called to cancel the change. Now you need to refresh the Grid so that the user can see the new row of data that's been added to the table, as shown in Figure 5-7.

Figure 5-7. A requeried table shows the new record in the Grid.

You may wonder how I got the new data to display without building and executing a new query to reflect the addition. There's a nifty little method called Requery that allows you to call on the existing Recordset to accomplish that goal for you. With the Recordset requeried and flush with new data, you display that data in the Grid using the new data and metadata discovery techniques that you learned using the Fields Collection.

Updating Data

I mentioned earlier in the book that one of the glaring holes in the Pocket SQL DML is the missing UPDATE statement. The Recordset object partially fills this gap with the Update method. This Update method doesn't actually do the same thing as the UPDATE statement, but it helps you do the same job nonetheless. You just witnessed how the Update method is called to commit a new row of records to the database when using the AddNew method. Well, the Update method can be used to commit a change to a record based on a simple edit. The only downside is that you can only edit and change one record at a time, whereas the UPDATE statement can make large changes to an unlimited number of records based on an appropriate query. Let's take a look at a simple edit to see how it works in practice. Drag a CommandButton from the Toolbox and drop it on your form. Name this control "cmdUpdate" and set its caption to read "Update." In the click event of this CommandButton, insert the following code:

```
Private Sub cmdUpdate_Click()

        'Declare variables
        Dim i As Integer
        Dim FirstName As String
        Dim LastName As String
        Dim CompanyName As String
        Dim StreetAddress As String
        Dim City As String
        Dim State As String
        Dim Zip As String
        Dim ColumnNames As String
        Dim ColumnValues As String


        'Get user input
        FirstName = InputBox("Enter a First Name", "Edit")
        LastName = InputBox("Enter a Last Name", "Edit")
        CompanyName = InputBox("Enter a Company Name", "Edit")
        StreetAddress = InputBox("Enter a Street Address", "Edit")
        City = InputBox("Enter a City", "Edit")
        State = InputBox("Enter a State", "Edit")
        Zip = InputBox("Enter a Zip Code", "Edit")

        'check to see if there's any editing in progress
        If RS.EditMode <> adEditNone Then
```

```
            MsgBox "There's editing in progress. Try the operation again later."
            Exit Sub
    End If

    'Edit the current record
    RS("FirstName") = FirstName
    RS("LastName") = LastName
    RS("CompanyName") = CompanyName
    RS("StreetAddress") = StreetAddress
    RS("City") = City
    RS("State") = State
    RS("Zip") = Zip

    'Ask user if he or she wants the record modified
    If MsgBox("Do you wish to edit this record?", vbYesNoCancel) = vbYes Then
            RS.Update
    Else
            RS.CancelUpdate
            MsgBox "The record is unchanged."
    End If

    'Move off the record and then return to it
    RS.MoveNext
    RS.MovePrevious

    'Remove existing data from Grid
    For i = 1 To GridCtrl1.Rows
            GridCtrl1.RemoveItem 0
    Next

    'Set the Grid columns equal to the field count
    GridCtrl1.Cols = RS.Fields.Count

    'Get the column names
    For i = 0 To RS.Fields.Count - 1
            ColumnNames = ColumnNames & RS.Fields(i).Name & vbTab
    Next

    'Add the column headers to the Grid
    GridCtrl1.AddItem ColumnNames

    'Get the column values for this row
    For i = 0 To RS.Fields.Count - 1
```

```
        ColumnValues = ColumnValues & RS.Fields(i).Value & vbTab
    Next

    'Add the column values to the row
    GridCtrl1.AddItem ColumnValues

End Sub
```

This time when you run your program, select a particular row that you'd like to change by using the MoveFirst, MoveNext, MovePrevious, and MoveLast buttons. When you find the desired record, click the Update button. You'll see that the code behaves the same way that the AddNew code did in the last example. It asks you for new record information and then checks to make sure that nobody else is currently editing the record.

At this point, the code changes due to the fact that you don't call the AddNew method before setting the fields equal to your newly inputted data. This tells ADOCE that you just want to change the existing record rather than add a new one. The next bit of the code is similar to the AddNew code except that you don't requery the database; you instead call the MoveNext and MovePrevious methods in succession. The act of moving off the targeted record and then moving back to it enables you to see the change made to it. Finally, you use your data and metadata discovery code except that you have it just display the current record rather than the whole Recordset. Notice how I changed the new ContactID record 5 from Torgeir Mantor to Michelle Tyree, as shown in Figure 5-8.

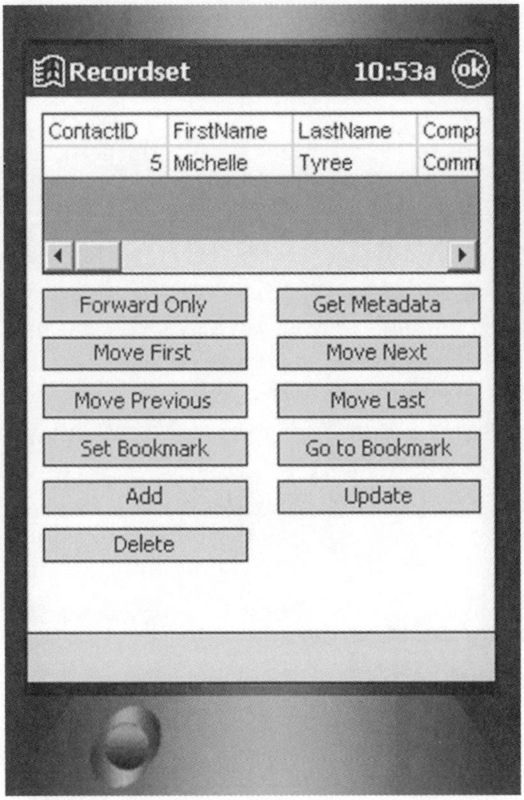

Figure 5-8. Record 5 has been changed.

Deleting Data

When you need to get rid of a row of data, the Recordset object provides its own
counterpart to the DML DELETE statement. The fact that it can only delete one
record at a time tells you that it suffers from the same limitations that restrict
your ability to edit multiple records using the Update method of the Recordset
object. The Delete method is simple to use, so let's build an example to illustrate
that fact. Drag a CommandButton from the Toolbox and drop it on your form.
Name this control "cmdDelete" and set its caption to read "Delete." In the click
event of this CommandButton, insert the following code:

```
Private Sub cmdDelete_Click()

        'Declare variables
        Dim i As Integer
        Dim ColumnNames As String
        Dim ColumnValues As String
```

```
'check to see if there's any editing in progress
If RS.EditMode <> adEditNone Then
        MsgBox "There's editing in progress. Try the operation again later."
        Exit Sub
End If

'Ask user if he or she wants the record deleted
If MsgBox("Do you wish to delete this record?", vbYesNoCancel) = vbYes Then
        RS.Delete
Else
        'RS.CancelUpdate
        MsgBox "The record is unchanged."
End If

'Move off the record and then return to it
RS.MoveNext
RS.MovePrevious

'Remove existing data from Grid
For i = 1 To GridCtrl1.Rows
        GridCtrl1.RemoveItem 0
Next

'Set the Grid columns equal to the field count
GridCtrl1.Cols = RS.Fields.Count

'Get the column names
For i = 0 To RS.Fields.Count - 1
        ColumnNames = ColumnNames & RS.Fields(i).Name & vbTab
Next

'Add the column headers to the Grid
GridCtrl1.AddItem ColumnNames

'Get the column values for this row
For i = 0 To RS.Fields.Count - 1
        ColumnValues = ColumnValues & RS.Fields(i).Value & vbTab
Next

'Add the column values to the row
GridCtrl1.AddItem ColumnValues


End Sub
```

You use this code in the same way that you used the Update code in the previous example. Move to the record that you want to delete and then click the Delete button. This time, your code doesn't ask for any data, but it still checks to see if someone else is editing the current record. It asks you if you really want to delete the record you've chosen and then calls the Delete method if you answer Yes. Otherwise, your Recordset is left unchanged. Finally, the Grid reflects the fact that the record you chose to delete is no longer there.

Summary

It's plain to see why the Recordset is the most frequently used object in ADOCE. Just about anything you want to do with a database can be done with the Recordset object. After reading five chapters covering the DDL, the DML, the Connection object, and the Recordset object, you now have the solid foundation required to build any kind of database application that you might need on the Pocket PC. It's now time to figure out how to keep your Pocket PC and desktop databases in sync.

CHAPTER 6

ActiveSync

IN CHAPTER 1, YOU DISCOVERED how to set up ActiveSync and you learned that it provides a conduit between your Pocket PC and your desktop computer. This conduit enables you to run your eMbedded Visual Basic applications on your Pocket PC and it allows you to synchronize things such as your Outlook e-mail, Web pages, files, and databases. Because this is a database book, I'm only going to focus on how ActiveSync enables you to keep desktop and handheld databases in sync with each other.

ActiveSync is a powerful feature with obvious benefits to business users of the Pocket PC. Many companies have mobile workforces that need to have vital corporate data available to them when they're out of the office or on the road. They need to be able to synchronize their Pocket PCs with desktop and corporate databases first thing in the morning so that they have the latest company information at their fingertips while out in the field. Likewise, new data that's captured on the Pocket PC by mobile workers needs to get back to corporate databases so that decisions can be made based on the new information. Professions that would find this technology useful include the following:

- **Real estate agents:** Every morning, a real estate agent can sync up with the MLS database to ensure that he or she has the latest information and photos of all the homes for sale in the area. Having the answers to potential homebuyer questions on the Pocket PC can enhance the agent's responsiveness and increase customer satisfaction.

- **Sales force personnel:** Offline client information on the Pocket PC combined with corporate database synchronization makes for a powerful sales force automation tool. New leads discovered in the field can turn into sales calls when data is replicated back to the office through the Internet or the USB cradle.

- **Doctors:** Rather than filling out patient charts and putting up with mounds of paperwork, doctors can now enter patient data on the Pocket PC and merge that data with hospital patient databases at the end of their shift. Pocket PC handwriting recognition can turn a doctor's illegible scribbling into accurate drug prescriptions.

- **Insurance agents:** When an insurance agent visits a client at his or her home, the agent can dispense with paper forms and enter insurance application information directly into the Pocket PC. The synching of new policy data can happen immediately using remote access or it can happen when the agent gets back to the office.

The list of uses for Pocket PC data that can replicate with corporate databases can go on and on. Let's stop talking about what can be done and start learning how to do it. The first thing I'll do is bore you with the details of data conversion between the desktop and the device so that you can make better decisions about the data types you choose to use. The next thing you're going to do is build an Access database on the desktop and then walk through the necessary steps to get that database on your Pocket PC and converted into Pocket Access format. You'll then build a full-featured DML Pocket Access database manager so you can add, delete, and update synchronized data to your heart's content. Finally, you'll play ping-pong with your data with lots of manipulation thrown in to prove that ActiveSync really works.

Data Conversion Issues

The movement of data between databases on your Pocket PC and your desktop is far from seamless. ActiveSync has its work cut out for it when trying to maintain the integrity of your data during the synchronization process.

Desktop to Device

Starting out on the desktop, ActiveSync can work with Microsoft Access or any ODBC-compliant database. It then has the unenviable task of converting your perfectly good desktop or server database into a Pocket Access database. With its small footprint, Pocket Access doesn't support the enterprise features or the range of data types that SQL Server or Oracle does. ActiveSync is forced to map data types, which may result in the loss of data if the data types don't match up well. Table 6-1 displays Access and ODBC data types and the Pocket Access types they map to.

Table 6-1. Desktop to Device Type Mappings

ACCESS DATA TYPE	ODBC DATA TYPE	POCKET ACCESS DATA TYPE
Text	sql_varchar	Varchar
Memo	sql_longvarchar	Text
LongInt	sql_integer	Integer
	sql_bigint	Integer
Byte	sql_tinyint	Smallint
Int	sql_smallint	Smallint
Single	sql_real	Double
Double	sql_double	Double
	sql_float	Double
ReplID	sql_varbinary	Varbinary
Date/Time	sql_timestamp	Datetime
Currency	sql_numeric	Double
AutoNumber	sql_integer	Integer
YesNo	sql_bit	Boolean
OleObject	sql_longvarbinary	Varbinary
HyperLink	sql_longvarchar	Text
Lookup	sql_varchar	Varchar

Table Issues

- A table will not be converted or copied to your Pocket PC if all its fields use unsupported data types.

- System tables will not be converted or copied to your Pocket PC.

- Table names longer than 31 characters will be truncated.

- If a table with a truncated name exists and you've chosen not to overwrite tables, the last character of that table name will be deleted and replaced with the number 0. If a truncated table name already has a 0, numbers 1 through 9 will be tried. If truncated tables exist with all ten numbers, the table won't be copied.

Field Issues

- Field names longer than 64 characters will be truncated.

Index Issues

- Index names longer than 64 characters will be truncated.

- Only Ascending and Descending index attributes will be copied. All other index attributes will be omitted.

- Only three indexes are allowed in a database. Indexes beyond that number will be skipped.

- Index names are not case sensitive.

- Only the first field of a multicolumn index will be indexed in Pocket Access.

- Pocket Access indexes are created in three stages during the conversion process.

Stage 1: Unique Primary Key Indexes

Any unique index named "PrimaryKey" will be processed first. If this is a single-field index, PrimaryKey will be created in Pocket Access. If PrimaryKey is made up of multiple fields, an index will be created for each field that exists in Pocket Access. If need be, these fields will have 0, 1, or 2 appended to their names. A Boolean cannot be a unique PrimaryKey index.

Stage 2: Unique Indexes

Unique indexes are created in Pocket Access after PrimaryKey indexes. If any of the following statements are true, a unique index will not be created.

- A 64-character, truncated index name matches an index name that is already present in Pocket Access.

- The particular field already has an index in Pocket Access.

- The indexed field is a Boolean data type.

Stage 3: Nonunique Indexes

Nonunique indexes are created after unique indexes. If any of the following statements are true, a nonunique index will not be created.

- The index contains more than one field.

- The indexed field is not selected to be copied to Pocket Access.

- A 64-character, truncated index name matches an index name that is already present in Pocket Access.

- The particular field already has an index in Pocket Access.

- The indexed field is a Boolean data type.

Device to Desktop

When moving from a Pocket Access database to a desktop Microsoft Access or ODBC database, things don't look as bad because you don't have to funnel countless desktop data types into a handful of device data types. The result is a reduced chance of data loss. Table 6–2 lists all the Pocket Access data types as well as the ODBC and Access data types that they map to.

Table 6-2. Device to Desktop Type Mappings

POCKET ACCESS DATA TYPE	ODBC DATA TYPE	ACCESS DATA TYPE
Datetime	sql_timestamp	Date/Time
Double	sql_double	Double
Integer	sql_integer	LongInt
Smallint	sql_smallint	int
Boolean	sql_bit	YesNo
Varbinary	sql_varbinary	Binary
Long Varbinary	sql_longvarbinary	OLEObject
Varchar	sql_varchar	Text
Text	sql_longvarchar	Memo

Table Issues

- A table will not be converted or copied to your desktop PC if the table is a system table.

- A table will not be converted or copied to your desktop PC if it doesn't have an entry in the MSysTables table.

Index Issues

- If the Pocket Access index has a name beginning with the text PrimaryKey, a unique index will be created on the desktop.

- Only Ascending and Descending index attributes will be copied. All other index attributes will be omitted.

Conversion Error Log

When ActiveSync is converting data between your desktop and your Pocket PC, both informational and fatal errors may occur. An informational error occurs when the structure of the data has to be altered as a result of things such as a truncated field or table name. A fatal error occurs when the data can no longer be copied to the desktop or Pocket PC as a result of a break in the communications link or some other anomaly. When either of these kinds of errors occurs, a log file named "Db2ce.txt" is generated in the device partner directory on the desktop PC. The information contained in the error log is displayed in Table 6-3.

Table 6-3. Conversion Error Log

SECTION	DESCRIPTION
Startup Statistics	Displays the user name, conversion start time, and the user options that were selected for conversion.
Desktop Computer Database	For Access databases, it displays which .mdb file is being copied and where it's located. For ODBC databases, it shows the connection string.
Options Chosen	Displays the sync or overwrite options chosen. Displays 1 for True and 0 for False.
Index Statistics	Displays information about converted indexes.
Table Statistics	Displays the SQL statement used to create the table and shows the number of records copied.
Closing Statistics	Displays the time the conversion was completed and the number of tables, records, packets, and bytes copied.

Even though this section on data conversion issues may not seem that interesting, it's important for you to take it seriously. Every time you build a desktop or ODBC database that you intend to sync your Pocket PC with, let the type mapping tables guide you. Your big database should only use data types that work well with your little database.

Shrinking a Database

Now it's time to dive in and see how you can put a single-user database synching relationship into production. The first thing you'll need to do is construct a simple database on your desktop computer. Let's stick with the simple contact manager database you've been using throughout the book as a model for your desktop database. My database of choice will be SQL Server 2000, which will communicate with ActiveSync through an ODBC connection.

TIP *If you don't have a copy of SQL Server 2000, download a 120-day evaluation copy from the Microsoft Web site (http://www.microsoft.com/sql/productinfo/evaluate.htm). Microsoft Access is also a perfectly acceptable partner in a single-user database relationship between your desktop and your Pocket PC when you work with ActiveSync.*

Building the Database

Bring up the SQL Server 2000 Enterprise Manager and create a new database called "ContactManager." Next, create a table in your new database called "Contacts." The column names, data types, and so on are listed in Table 6-4.

Table 6-4. Contacts Table Data Types

COLUMN NAME	DATA TYPE	LENGTH	ALLOW NULLS	IDENTITY (AUTO NUMBER)
ContactID	int	4	No	Yes
FirstName	varchar	50	Yes	No
LastName	varchar	50	Yes	No
CompanyName	varchar	50	Yes	No
StreetAddress	varchar	50	Yes	No
City	varchar	50	Yes	No
State	varchar	2	Yes	No
Zip	varchar	10	Yes	No

Make sure that the ContactID column is both the Key field and an Identity column in order to keep it unique. If you entered your data correctly, the resulting design view in the SQL Server Enterprise Manager should look like Figure 6-1.

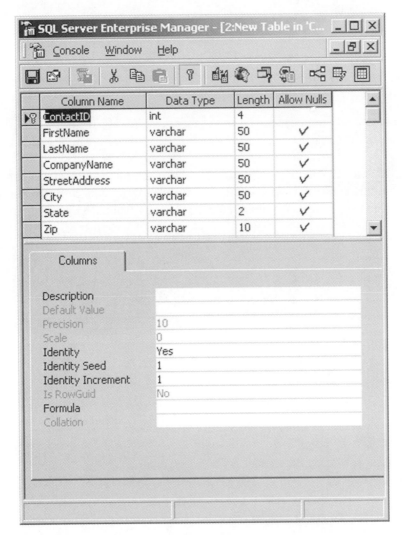

Figure 6-1. The Design view for the Contacts table

Now create the related PhoneNumbers table. The proper column names, data types, and so on are listed in Table 6-5.

Table 6-5. PhoneNumbers Table Data Types

COLUMN NAME	DATA TYPE	LENGTH	ALLOW NULLS	IDENTITY (AUTO NUMBER)
PhoneNumberID	int	4	No	Yes
ContactID	int	4	Yes	No
PhoneNumber	varchar	12	Yes	No

Make sure that the PhoneNumberID column is both the Key field and an Identity column in order to keep it unique. If you entered your data correctly, the resulting design view in the SQL Server Enterprise Manager should look like Figure 6-2.

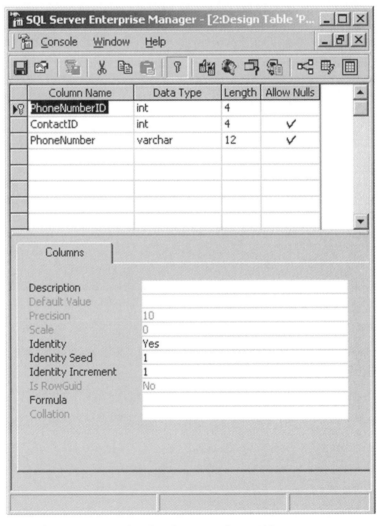

Figure 6-2. The Design view for the PhoneNumbers table

You won't create any explicit one-to-many relationships with the two tables because Pocket Access would ignore the referential integrity rules anyway. Now that you have your ContactManager database and tables constructed, you need to do one more thing before initiating the synching process. Word has it on many of the eMbedded Visual Basic Web sites and newsgroups that your desktop database needs to have at least one row of data entered into it before you run ActiveSync in order to consistently achieve good results. It's not a hard and fast requirement, but having that first row inserted will help you measure success or failure when you view the Pocket Access version of your ContactManager database. Go ahead and enter your own personal contact information into the Contacts table. The value of your ContactID Identity column should be 1 after you've inserted the row of data. Now go to the PhoneNumbers table and enter two phone numbers for yourself. Even though the PhoneNumberID Identity column will autoincrement its numbers, you will need to manually enter the ContactID that was assigned to you in the Contacts table for each phone number that you enter for yourself. Make sure your PhoneNumbers table looks something like Figure 6-3.

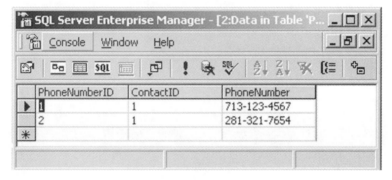

Figure 6-3. The Data view for the PhoneNumbers table

With your desktop database all set and ready to go, you need to create an ODBC DSN for your SQL Server 2000 ContactManager database. Bring up the ODBC Data Source Administrator, click the User DSN tab, and then click the Add button. Highlight SQL Server in the list box and click Finish. On the next screen, type in **Contact-Manager** for the name, choose (local) from the Server combo box, and then click Next. On the next screen, choose SQL Server Authentication, type in the appropriate login ID and password (with no password if you're bad), and click Next. Check the option Change the default database to, select ContactManager from the combo box, and then click Next. On the next screen, click Finish. On the last screen, click Test Data Source and then click OK twice if everything worked out with your data connection. Now you're ready for ActiveSync.

ActiveSync Walk-through

If you'll remember back to Chapter 1, I had you check Pocket Access as one of the programs to be synchronized between the desktop and the device. Now you're going to do just that. The other thing I mentioned back in Chapter 1 was that I would make every attempt to ensure that all of the examples in this book could be done with just the emulator. This chapter is going to be the exception because ActiveSync can only work against a real device.

With your Pocket PC sitting in its cradle and actively connected, bring up ActiveSync and select Tools ➤ Import Database Tables (as you see shown in Figure 6-4) to get started with converting your SQL Server database into a Pocket Access database.

Figure 6-4. Selecting Import Database Tables from the Tools menu

The next thing you'll see is an Open dialog box that enables you to navigate to your desktop database. Its default setting is to look for Microsoft Access databases. Go to the Files of type combo box and select ODBC Database. A Select Data Source dialog box opens for you to select a DSN. Click the Machine Data Source tab, select ContactManager from the list box, and then click OK. When the SQL Server Login dialog box opens, uncheck Use Trusted Connection, type in the appropriate entries in the Login ID and Password text boxes, and then click OK. You'll briefly see a Copy & Convert dialog box as your SQL Server data is imported. When the import is complete, the Import from Database to Mobile Device dialog box will appear, as shown in Figure 6-5.

 NOTE *I don't recommend using the Export Database Tables feature of ActiveSync to create a relationship between a Pocket Access database and a desktop database. This feature takes a Pocket Access database and converts it into a desktop database. Unfortunately, the source database on your Pocket PC only supports a small subset of the features and data types that a desktop or server database supports. This will leave you with a crippled desktop ActiveSync partner that's unable to perform even simple tasks, such as autoincrementing an indexed column.*

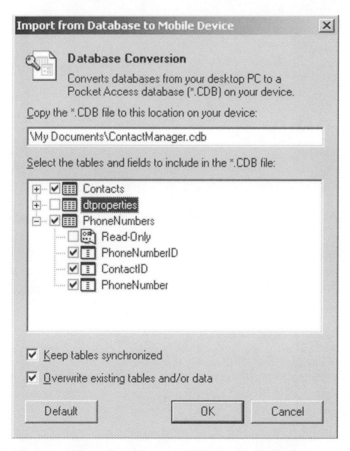

Figure 6-5. The Import from Database to Mobile Device dialog box

In this dialog box, you will specify all aspects of the synchronization relationship between SQL Server and Pocket Access. The text box at the top informs you that it plans to put your ContactManager Pocket Access database in the My Documents folder. This is a good place for your database, but you're free to change the location if you want. A Treeview displays the tables you created and every once in a while it displays a rogue system table called "dtproperties" that you have no interest in. Here you're allowed to select the tables you want converted. You can even decide to select specific fields if you don't want to convert the whole table. Finally, you're given the choice of selecting the Read Only option for each table if you don't want your Pocket Access database to be modified. Under the Treeview, don't change the default settings for keeping the tables synchronized and overwriting existing tables. Make sure that the only tables selected are Contacts and PhoneNumbers and then click OK to get things started. A Copy & Convert dialog box displays, as shown in Figure 6-6, to let you know that the conversion is under way.

Figure 6-6. Database conversion in progress

To verify the existence of the new Pocket Access database, bring up the File Explorer in your Pocket PC and look for a file named "ContactManager" located in the My Documents folder, as shown in Figure 6-7.

Figure 6-7. File Explorer displaying ContactManager

From now on, every time you return your Pocket PC to its cradle, it automatically synchronizes with the desktop database. Furthermore, you can manually synchronize your desktop and Pocket PC databases anytime you want by clicking the Sync button. Now that you've found the file, you need a flexible way to open and manipulate it. This sounds like a golden opportunity to write some code.

The Database Manipulator

Having the new Pocket Access database on your Pocket PC is only half the battle. You need to see for yourself that you can make additions, updates, and deletions on your Pocket PC and then see those changes reflected in your desktop database the next time you run ActiveSync. You're going to build an eMbedded Visual Basic program to do just that. This time around, you're not going to write code that's specific to the database that you're expecting. Throughout the book, I've made references to building a complete Pocket Access database manager that will give you DDL and DML features similar to what you're used to having in Microsoft Access 2000. In this chapter, you'll build a small piece of the program that will enable you to make additions, updates, and deletions to any Pocket Access database you like. It's about time we wrote a flexible program around here!

Bring up eMbedded Visual Basic and create a new project called "InSync." Check a reference to the Microsoft CE ADO Control 3.0 and add both the Common Dialog control and the Grid control to your project. Finally, add a Module to your project and call it "Module1."

Declaring Globals

Go to your Module and declare public object variables for both the ADOCE Connection object and the Recordset object. Additionally, declare a String variable to maintain the path to whatever Pocket Access database you choose to open.

```
Option Explicit

Public CN As ADOCE.Connection
Public RS As ADOCE.Recordset

Public PocketAccessDatabase As String
```

Instantiating Globals

In the Load event of your main form, you need to add the code necessary to instantiate both the Connection and the Recordset objects.

```
Private Sub Form_Load()

    'Instantiate the Connection Object
    Set CN = CreateObject("ADOCE.Connection.3.0")

    'Instantiate the Recordset Object
    Set RS = CreateObject("ADOCE.Recordset.3.0")

End Sub
```

Closing and Dereferencing Globals

In the OKClick event of your main form, you need to add code to close the Connection object as well as code to dereference both the Connection object and the Recordset object.

```
Private Sub Form_OKClick()

    If CN.State = 1 Then 'Open
        'Let's close the database
        CN.Close
    End If

    'Dereference the Recordset
    Set RS = Nothing

    'Dereference the Connection
    Set CN = Nothing

    App.End

End Sub
```

Opening and Closing the Database

Now things start to get interesting. You need to have a button that enables you to toggle between opening and closing your Pocket Access database. In order to actually open the database, you'll need the Common Dialog control to enable a user to navigate to and open Pocket Access database files. Therefore, you need to drag the Common Dialog control from the Toolbox and drop it on your form. This code also uses a Grid control as well as a combo box, so drag both of those items from the Toolbox and drop them on your form. Name the combo box "cboTableSelect" and set its Text property to "Select a Table." The Grid control can keep its default name and no property adjustments are necessary. To implement the code necessary to open and close the database, drag a CommandButton from the Toolbox and drop it on your form. Name this control "cmdOpenDatabase" and set its caption to read "Open Database." In the click event of this CommandButton, insert the following code:

```
Private Sub cmdOpenDatabase_Click()

    Select Case cmdOpenDatabase.Caption
        Case "Open Database"

            Dim fileflags As FileOpenConstants
            Dim e As Variant
            Dim i As Integer
```

```
'Set the text in the dialog box title bar
CommonDialog1.DialogTitle = "Open Database"

'Set the default filename and filter
CommonDialog1.InitDir = "\"
CommonDialog1.FileName = ""
CommonDialog1.Filter = "Pocket Access (*.cdb)|*.cdb"

'Verify that the file exists
CommonDialog1.Flags = cdlOFNFileMustExist

'Show the Open common dialog box
CommonDialog1.ShowOpen

'Return the path and filename selected or
'Return an empty string if the user cancels the dialog box
PocketAccessDatabase = CommonDialog1.FileName

If PocketAccessDatabase <> "" Then

    'Open the database
    CN.Open PocketAccessDatabase

    'Display Connection Errors
    For Each e In CN.Errors
        MsgBox e.Description
    Next

    'Display Tables
    RS.Open "MSysTables", CN
    While Not RS.EOF

        'Disregard all System Tables
        If RS("TableName") <> "MSysTables" _
        And RS("TableName") <> "MSysIndexes" _
        And RS("TableName") <> "MSysFields" _
        And RS("TableName") <> "MSysProcs" Then
            'Add table to combo box
            cboTableSelect.AddItem RS("TableName")
        End If
```

```
                RS.MoveNext
            Wend

            RS.Close

            'Change caption
            cmdOpenDatabase.Caption = "Close Database"

        End If

    Case "Close Database"

        If CN.State = 1 Then 'Open
            'Let's close the database
            CN.Close
        End If

        'Remove existing data from Grid
        GridCtrl1.Redraw = False
        For i = 1 To GridCtrl1.Rows
            GridCtrl1.RemoveItem 0
        Next
        GridCtrl1.Redraw = True

        'Clear the combo box
        cboTableSelect.Clear

        'Reset combo box text
        cboTableSelect.Text = "Select a Table"

        'Zero out the path to the database
        PocketAccessDatabase = ""

        'Change caption
        cmdOpenDatabase.Caption = "Open Database"

    End Select


End Sub
```

The beginning of this block of code starts out with a Case statement based on the value of the CommandButton caption. If the caption reads "Open Database," you execute the appropriate code to get the database loaded into your program. On the other hand, if the caption reads "Close Database," you execute the code necessary to unload the database from your program. The next bit of code deals with the Common Dialog control. You set its filter to ensure that it only looks for files that end in .cdb. You also set a flag that makes sure that the file you're trying to open truly exists. Once the Common Dialog is open and the user has chosen the database they want to open, set the PocketAccessDatabase string equal to the path given to you by the Common Dialog control. Based on that path, you open a database connection and then proceed to list all the tables in the database in a combo box. The last bit of code is concerned with closing the database and performing cleanup operations, such as clearing out the Grid and combo box.

Choosing a Table

Once the database is open, the combo box named "cboTableSelect" is filled with the names of the tables in the database. Selecting one of these tables from the combo box will cause the Grid to be filled with the metadata and data associated with the selected table. In order to make this happen, insert the following code in the click event of this combo box:

```
Private Sub cboTableSelect_Click()

    'Declare variables
    Dim i As Integer
    Dim ColumnNames As String
    Dim ColumnValues As String

    'A keyset-based, forward and backward, read and write Recordset
    RS.Open cboTableSelect.List(cboTableSelect.ListIndex), CN, adOpenKeyset,
    adLockOptimistic, adCmdTable

    'Remove existing data from Grid
    GridCtrl1.Redraw = False
    For i = 1 To GridCtrl1.Rows
        GridCtrl1.RemoveItem 0
    Next
    GridCtrl1.Redraw = True

    'Set the Grid columns equal to the field count
    GridCtrl1.Cols = RS.Fields.Count
```

```
'Get the column names
For i = 0 To RS.Fields.Count - 1
    ColumnNames = ColumnNames & RS.Fields(i).Name & vbTab
Next

GridCtrl1.Redraw = False

'Add the column headers to the Grid
GridCtrl1.AddItem ColumnNames

'Loop through the Recordset
While Not RS.EOF

    'Get the column values for this row
    For i = 0 To RS.Fields.Count - 1
        ColumnValues = ColumnValues & RS.Fields(i).Value & vbTab
    Next

    'Add the column values to the row
    GridCtrl1.AddItem ColumnValues

    'Set ColumnValues to a zero-length string
    'so it can be refilled with the next row
    ColumnValues = ""

    RS.MoveNext
Wend

GridCtrl1.Redraw = True

'Close the Recordset
RS.Close

End Sub
```

The first thing that happens in this block of code is that a Recordset is opened based on the name of the table you selected from the combo box. This Recordset is designed to return all the columns from the table in question. The next thing you'll notice is that I've added some new code to complement the standard Grid-clearing code. At the beginning of the operation, I set the Grid's Redraw property to False and then I set it back to True once all the rows have been removed. Doing this causes the Grid to both clear and fill with data much faster. You may not notice a performance difference in your emulator, but you sure can see a difference when you run the application on your Pocket PC. The next thing that happens is that you iterate through and dynamically display the column names as well as the column values for each row. Finally, you close the Recordset.

Adding a Record

Now that you have a Grid full of data based on the table you've chosen, you may want to add an additional record to it. In order to do this, you should drag a CommandButton from the Toolbox and drop it on your form. Name this control "cmdAdd" and set its caption to read "Add a Record." In the click event of this CommandButton, insert the following code:

```
Private Sub cmdAdd_Click()

    cmdAdd.Enabled = False

    'Declare variables
    Dim i As Integer
    Dim ColumnNames As String
    Dim ColumnValues As String

    'A keyset-based, forward and backward, read and write Recordset
    RS.Open cboTableSelect.List(cboTableSelect.ListIndex), CN, adOpenKeyset,
    adLockOptimistic, adCmdTable

    'Call the AddNew method
    RS.AddNew

    'Get dynamic user input
    For i = 0 To RS.Fields.Count - 1

        'If the field is an integer. . .
        If RS.Fields(i).Type = adInteger Then

            'Ask the user if the field is autoincrementing
            If MsgBox("Is " & RS.Fields(i).Name & " an autoincrementing field?",
            vbYesNoCancel) = vbYes Then

                'Code to Auto Increment
                Dim AutoNumber As Integer
                Dim Identity As ADOCE.Recordset
                Set Identity = CreateObject("ADOCE.Recordset.3.0")
```

```
              Identity.Open "SELECT " & RS.Fields(i).Name & " FROM " &
cboTableSelect.List(cboTableSelect.ListIndex) & " ORDER BY " &
              RS.Fields(i).Name & " DESC", CN
              If Not RS.BOF And Not RS.EOF Then
                  AutoNumber = CInt(Identity(0)) + 1
              Else
                  AutoNumber = 1
              End If
              Identity.Close
              Set Identity = Nothing

              'Set new field equal to a new autoincremented number
              RS(RS.Fields(i).Name) = AutoNumber

          Else

              'Set new field equal to user input
              RS(RS.Fields(i).Name) = InputBox(RS.Fields(i).Name, "Add")

          End If

      Else

          'Set new field equal to user input
          RS(RS.Fields(i).Name) = InputBox(RS.Fields(i).Name, "Add")

      End If

  Next

  'Ask user if he or she wants the record added
  If MsgBox("Do you wish to add this record?", vbYesNoCancel) = vbYes Then
      RS.Update
  Else
      RS.CancelUpdate
      MsgBox "No new record added."
  End If

  'Query the database again to refresh the Grid
  RS.Requery

  'Remove existing data from Grid
  GridCtrl1.Redraw = False
  For i = 1 To GridCtrl1.Rows
```

```vb
        GridCtrl1.RemoveItem 0
    Next
    GridCtrl1.Redraw = True

    'Set the Grid columns equal to the field count
    GridCtrl1.Cols = RS.Fields.Count

    'Get the column names
    For i = 0 To RS.Fields.Count - 1
        ColumnNames = ColumnNames & RS.Fields(i).Name & vbTab
    Next

    GridCtrl1.Redraw = False

    'Add the column headers to the grid
    GridCtrl1.AddItem ColumnNames

    'Loop through the Recordset
    While Not RS.EOF

        'Get the column values for this row
        For i = 0 To RS.Fields.Count - 1
            ColumnValues = ColumnValues & RS.Fields(i).Value & vbTab
        Next

        'Add the column values to the row
        GridCtrl1.AddItem ColumnValues

        'Set ColumnValues to a zero-length string
        'so it can be refilled with the next row
        ColumnValues = ""

        RS.MoveNext

    Wend

    GridCtrl1.Redraw = True

    RS.Close

    cmdAdd.Enabled = True

End Sub
```

When you learned how to add a record to a table back in Chapter 5, you knew the table structure in advance and therefore wrote rigid code based on that fact. Because everything about the program here in Chapter 6 is dynamic, the code is a lot trickier. Your code block starts out normally enough with the opening of a Recordset based on the currently selected table. After you call the AddNew method, things start to get a little crazy. The goal is to pop up Input boxes to ask the user to type in the new record data. The problem is that you don't know the names of the table columns in advance of doing so. As a result, you have to iterate through the Fields Collection to determine the column names that the user is entering data into—but don't get too cozy just yet.

What do you do about those pesky autoincrementing indexes that work on the desktop but not on the Pocket PC? The workaround is to check the data type of each column as you iterate through the Fields Collection. When you find an Integer data type, you prompt the user with a Yes/No message box and ask if the field is autoincrementing. Don't worry, when you build your Pocket Access database manager in the next chapter, I promise to be more scientific about the determination of autoincrementing fields. Anyway, if the user chooses Yes, you open up a second Recordset to figure out the highest number in the given field and add 1 to that number to get your new AutoNumber value. If the user chooses No, you prompt the user to enter his or her own Integer in an Input Box.

After getting all the non-Integer user inputs, you ask the user if he or she is sure he or she wants to add this new record. If the user chooses Yes, you call the Update method. If the user chooses No, you call the CancelUpdate method. The rest of the code is similar to what you've done before. You'll empty the Grid and then dynamically refill it to display the new record.

NOTE *Because there's no referential integrity enforcement in Pocket Access, you'll have to follow up on adding, updating, and deleting records in related tables manually.*

Updating a Record

The second DML function you'll want to perform after adding records is updating records. For the purposes of this program, I'll allow you to click any cell in the Grid and let you update the contents of that cell. To accomplish this tall order, drag a CommandButton from the Toolbox and drop it on your form. Name this control "cmdUpdate" and set its caption to read "Update the Selected Record." In the click event of this CommandButton, insert the following code:

```
Private Sub cmdUpdate_Click()
```

```
'Declare variables
Dim i As Integer
Dim ColumnNames As String
Dim ColumnValues As String
Dim SQL As String

If GridCtrl1.RowSel > 0 Then

    If GridCtrl1.TextMatrix(GridCtrl1.RowSel, GridCtrl1.ColSel) <> "" Then

        'Build a query to return just the column and value
        'reflected in the user's Grid selection
        SQL = "SELECT " & GridCtrl1.TextMatrix(0, GridCtrl1.ColSel) &
        " FROM " & cboTableSelect.List(cboTableSelect.ListIndex) & " WHERE " &
        GridCtrl1.TextMatrix(0, GridCtrl1.ColSel) & " = " &
        GridCtrl1.TextMatrix(GridCtrl1.RowSel, GridCtrl1.ColSel)

        'A keyset-based, forward and backward, read and write Recordset
        RS.Open SQL, CN, adOpenKeyset, adLockOptimistic, adCmdText

        'Get dynamic user input
        For i = 0 To RS.Fields.Count - 1

            'Set new field equal to user input
            RS(RS.Fields(i).Name) = InputBox(RS.Fields(i).Name, "Add")

        Next

        'Ask user if he or she wants the record added
        If MsgBox("Do you wish to update this record?", vbYesNoCancel) = vbYes
Then
            RS.Update
        Else
            RS.CancelUpdate
            MsgBox "No new record updated."
        End If

        RS.Close

        'Query the database again to refresh the Grid
        'A keyset-based, forward and backward, read and write Recordset
        RS.Open cboTableSelect.List(cboTableSelect.ListIndex), CN,
        adOpenKeyset, adLockOptimistic, adCmdTable
```

```
'Remove existing data from Grid
GridCtrl1.Redraw = False
For i = 1 To GridCtrl1.Rows
    GridCtrl1.RemoveItem 0
Next
GridCtrl1.Redraw = True

'Set the Grid columns equal to the field count
GridCtrl1.Cols = RS.Fields.Count

'Get the column names
For i = 0 To RS.Fields.Count - 1
    ColumnNames = ColumnNames & RS.Fields(i).Name & vbTab
Next

GridCtrl1.Redraw = False

'Add the column headers to the Grid
GridCtrl1.AddItem ColumnNames

'Loop through the Recordset
While Not RS.EOF

    'Get the column values for this row
    For i = 0 To RS.Fields.Count - 1
        ColumnValues = ColumnValues & RS.Fields(i).Value & vbTab
    Next

    'Add the column values to the row
    GridCtrl1.AddItem ColumnValues

    'Set ColumnValues to a zero-length string
    'so it can be refilled with the next row
    ColumnValues = ""

    RS.MoveNext

Wend

GridCtrl1.Redraw = True

RS.Close
```

```
              End If

       End If

End Sub
```

The first thing that happens at the top of the code block is you make sure that your Update code is only executed if the user selects a nonmetadata row in the Grid. The next thing you have to do is build a complicated SQL statement using the TextMatrix property of the Grid that determines the column name as well as the value of the cell selected by the user. You open a Recordset that contains a single column and a single row to update. You then dynamically prompt the user to enter the new value for this cell. After that, you call the Update or CancelUpdate method depending on whether or not the user wants to commit the change to the database. The final bit of code refreshes the Grid so that you can see the results of the cell update.

Deleting a Record

The Delete function in this program works similarly to the Update function. When a user clicks a cell in the Grid, the row that cell belongs to is deleted. To make this operation a reality, drag a CommandButton from the Toolbox and drop it on your form. Name this control "cmdDelete" and set its caption to read "Delete the Selected Record." In the click event of this CommandButton, insert the following code:

```
Private Sub cmdDelete_Click()

    'Declare variables
    Dim i As Integer
    Dim ColumnNames As String
    Dim ColumnValues As String
    Dim SQL As String

    If GridCtrl1.RowSel > 0 Then

        If GridCtrl1.TextMatrix(GridCtrl1.RowSel, GridCtrl1.ColSel) <> "" Then

            SQL = "SELECT * FROM " & cboTableSelect.List(cboTableSelect.ListIndex) &
                " WHERE " & GridCtrl1.TextMatrix(0, GridCtrl1.ColSel) & " = " &
                GridCtrl1.TextMatrix(GridCtrl1.RowSel, GridCtrl1.ColSel)

            'A keyset-based, forward and backward, read and write Recordset
```

```
        RS.Open SQL, CN, adOpenKeyset, adLockOptimistic, adCmdText

    'Ask user if he or she wants the record deleted
    If MsgBox("Do you wish to delete this record?", vbYesNoCancel) = vbYes Then

        RS.Delete

        RS.Close

        'Query the database again to refresh the Grid
        'A keyset-based, forward and backward, read and write Recordset
        RS.Open cboTableSelect.List(cboTableSelect.ListIndex), CN,
        adOpenKeyset, adLockOptimistic, adCmdTable

        'Remove existing data from Grid
        GridCtrl1.Redraw = False
        For i = 1 To GridCtrl1.Rows
            GridCtrl1.RemoveItem 0
        Next
        GridCtrl1.Redraw = True

        'Set the Grid columns equal to the field count
        GridCtrl1.Cols = RS.Fields.Count

        'Get the column names
        For i = 0 To RS.Fields.Count - 1
            ColumnNames = ColumnNames & RS.Fields(i).Name & vbTab
        Next

        GridCtrl1.Redraw = False

        'Add the column headers to the Grid
        GridCtrl1.AddItem ColumnNames

        'Loop through the Recordset
        While Not RS.EOF

            'Get the column values for this row
            For i = 0 To RS.Fields.Count - 1
                ColumnValues = ColumnValues & RS.Fields(i).Value & vbTab
            Next

            'Add the column values to the row
            GridCtrl1.AddItem ColumnValues
```

```
                          'Set ColumnValues to a zero-length string
                          'so it can be refilled with the next row
                          ColumnValues = ""

                          RS.MoveNext
                     Wend
                     GridCtrl1.Redraw = True

             Else

                     MsgBox "The record is unchanged."
             End If
             RS.Close
        End If
    End If

End Sub
```

After checking to make sure that the user doesn't click a metadata cell in the Grid, a complicated SQL string is constructed with the help of the Grid's TextMatrix property. This query causes the Recordset to open only the row of data the user clicked on in the Grid. The user is then prompted with a Yes/No message box asking whether or not to delete the selected record. If the user chooses Yes, the Delete method is called and the code proceeds to refresh the Grid so you can see that the row in question has been removed.

Trying It Out

Now that you've wired all this code together, it's time to see what your little program can do. By the way, you can put your Grid, combo box, and buttons anywhere you want, but mine looks like Figure 6-8.

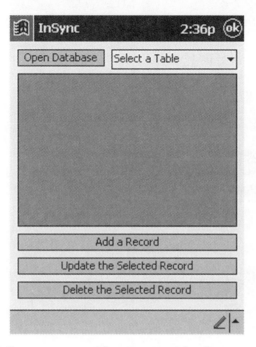

Figure 6-8. The InSync program without an open database

You're about to start playing ping-pong with your data as you bounce it from Pocket Access to SQL Server. The InSync program in conjunction with the SQL Server Enterprise Manager will help you accomplish the following tasks:

- Verify the original conversion and row of data

- Add data to Pocket Access

- Update data in SQL Server

- Update data in Pocket Access

- Delete data in SQL Server

- Delete data in Pocket Access

Bring up the InSync program on your Pocket PC so you can get started putting it through its paces.

Verifying Original Conversion and Row of Data

The first thing you need to do is verify that the database you built and the row of data you added in SQL Server has made it to your Pocket PC successfully. Click the Open Database button to display the Open common dialog box. It should default to All Folders and should display only files that end in .cdb, as you see shown in Figure 6-9.

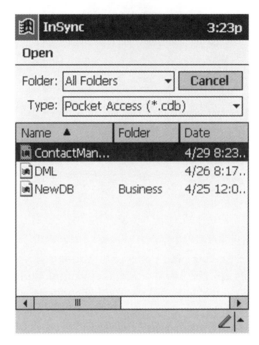

Figure 6-9. The Open common dialog box displaying the ContactManager database

Hopefully, you'll see your ContactManager database. Tap on the database to open it. The next thing you need to do is click the Select a Table combo box (see Figure 6-10) and choose the Contacts table.

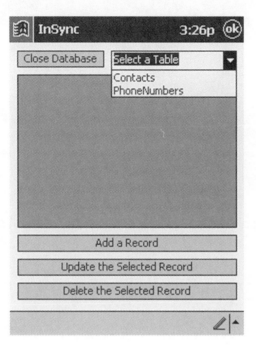

Figure 6-10. Select a table

Once you've clicked Contacts, the Grid should fill with the same metadata and data you entered in SQL Server. Your Grid should look something like Figure 6-11.

Figure 6-11. The Grid displaying the Contacts table

Be sure that you also verify the contents of the PhoneNumbers table as well before you move on.

Adding Data in Pocket Access

Now you get to try out your Add a Record function and see how its dynamic adding capabilities work. Reselect the Contacts table from the combo box so that it's displayed in the Grid. Now click the Add a Record button to start the process. As your code loops through the metadata, it should display the message box shown in Figure 6-12 almost immediately.

Figure 6-12. Checking for autoincrementing fields

Because you created ContactID as an Identity column in SQL Server, you know that it is an autoincrementing field and you should therefore click Yes. From there on, you will see a series of Input Boxes prompting you to enter values for the given column name as shown in Figure 6-13.

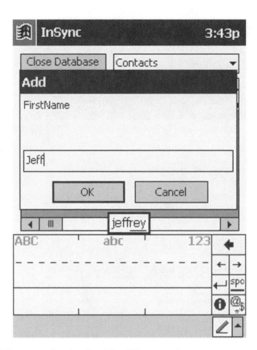

Figure 6-13. Adding a value in the FirstName column

After you've entered all the necessary data for this new record, click Yes when you're asked if you want to add the record. If all went well, you should be looking at a new row of data in your Grid with a ContactID of 2. Now I want you to close the database but leave InSync running. Go to ActiveSync on your desktop and click the Sync button. Once it's finished synchronizing, take a look at your Contacts table in SQL Server through the Enterprise Manager. It should look just like your InSync Grid looked a moment ago (mine did).

Updating Data in SQL Server

With the Contacts table displayed in the Enterprise Manager, change the last name of ContactID 2 by clicking in the cell and making the edit. Now close the Contacts table Grid, bring up ActiveSync and click the Sync button. When the synchronization is complete, go back to the InSync program on your Pocket PC, open the ContactManager database, and view the Contacts table in the Grid. Sure enough, your ContactID 2 should have a new last name. Mine went from Swantkowski to Johnston—try and top that!

Updating Data in Pocket Access

Not to be outdone by SQL Server, let's do some updating with Pocket Access. With the Contacts table displayed in the InSync Grid, tap the FirstName of ContactID 1. The cell should have a dotted outline around it signifying that it has been selected. Now click the Update the Selected Record button. If everything is working correctly, it should only prompt you to enter a new FirstName. When a message box asks if you want to update the record, tap the Yes button. You should now be looking at a refreshed Grid with a new FirstName for ContactID 1. This time, I changed my name from Rob to my wife's name, Cathy. I guess I'll inform her that she's the new CTO over at CommonVision. Now let's find out if Cathy survives the trip back to SQL Server. Close the InSync database and click the Sync button in ActiveSync. Display the Contacts table in the SQL Server Enterprise Manager and see if your Pocket Access change is reflected in SQL Server. In my case, my wife's name managed to beam over to SQL Server without any loss of molecular structure.

Deleting Data in SQL Server

It's now time for one of the two remaining contestants in the Contacts table to get voted out. In the Contacts table Grid in the Enterprise Manager, select the entire row of ContactID 1 and push the Delete key on your keyboard. With only contestant number two remaining, click the Sync button in ActiveSync. When the synchronization is finished, go back to your InSync program on your Pocket PC, open the ContactManager database, and select the Contacts table. If your code is working as good as mine, you should only see ContactID 2 displayed in the Grid.

Deleting Data in Pocket Access

Because no one gets out of this world alive, it's time to delete the remaining row of data in your Contacts table. Tap any one of the cells in ContactID 2's row so that the cell is outlined with dots. Now click the Delete the Selected Record button and definitely tap the Yes button when asked if you want to delete this record. You should now be staring at a Grid displaying only column metadata. Well, let's try to replicate your empty table back to SQL Server. Close the database on the Pocket PC and click the Sync button in ActiveSync. When the synchronization finishes, bring up the Contacts table Grid in the Enterprise Manager. If you did it right, your Grid should be empty with the exception of column metadata, as shown in Figure 6-14.

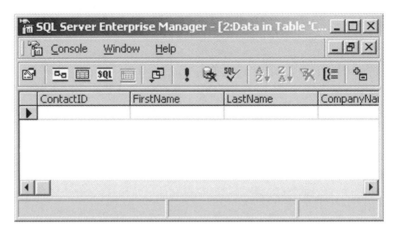

Figure 6-14. An empty table

Now that you've accomplished the previous tasks, you should feel confident in your ability to build single-user Pocket PC database applications that use ActiveSync. You've learned all the important points regarding establishing a relationship between a desktop or server database and a Pocket Access database. What about multiuser ActiveSync database relationships, you might ask? It's important to differentiate what you've done in this chapter with single-user issues versus what might happen in multiuser scenarios and how best to handle those issues. The single-user scenario assumes that only you are using the desktop and Pocket PC databases at any given time. When you're at your desk, only you make additions, updates, and deletions to your desktop database, whether that's Microsoft Access or SQL Server. This scenario also dictates that you'll run ActiveSync to replicate those changes to your Pocket PC *before* you decide to modify the data residing in Pocket Access. Likewise, when you're on the road making additions, updates, and deletions to your Pocket Access database, you must run ActiveSync upon your return to the office to replicate those changes to your desktop database *before* you decide to modify the data residing in Microsoft Access or SQL Server. At this point, you're probably wondering what the big deal is.

In a multiuser scenario, all kinds of people back at your office can make additions, updates, and deletions to your Microsoft Access or SQL Server database while you're on the road with your Pocket PC, and that *is* a big deal. At a minimum, you can just imagine the conflicts that will arise with your autoincrementing fields when you're making additions to Pocket Access while others are making additions to your desktop database at the same time. You'll end up with clashing Identity column numbers that ActiveSync won't be able to resolve and will therefore not synchronize. Go ahead and try this out for yourself by adding a new record to both your desktop and your Pocket Access databases. With new records added in both places with differing data but the same ID number, run ActiveSync to see what happens. You're now staring at an ActiveSync dialog box reporting the database synchronization conflict that it's going to write to its error log. I know you're hoping that I'm about to show you a slick workaround for this issue, but sadly, Pocket Access is now officially out of its league. Replication usually involves moving from autoincrementing key fields to using randomly generated numbers to uniquely identify a particular row. The only way to be certain that you won't have any conficting key fields is to use 128-bit GUIDs as your key field data type. The ability to autogenerate GUIDs for a key field whenever a new row is added is supported in SQL Server and Access but unfortunately not in Pocket Access. Since I don't know of a way to make the CoCreateGuid call work on the Pocket PC, you wouldn't even be able to generate the GUIDs yourself like you do with the autoincrementing numbers. Don't throw in the towel just yet, there is a solution.

Sophisticated data merge and replication code is used all the time in enterprise products such as Lotus Notes, Oracle, and Microsoft SQL Server. Using the right tools for the job can solve your multiuser replication issues. Those tools are SQL Server 2000, Windows 2000, Internet Information Server 5, and SQL Server CE 1.1. Firewall-friendly HTTP is used as the transport mechanism to replicate changes from SQL Server CE on your Pocket PC to SQL Server 2000 through IIS 5. Best of all, using merge replication, these products are designed to automatically handle the conflicts that arise in multiuser scenarios where the SQL Server 2000 database is being modified at the same time as the SQL Server CE database that's out on the road. I won't delve into SQL Server CE any further because it deserves its own book and this is a book on Pocket Access, but I would like to point you in the right direction to help you get started if you require this greater level of database sophistication. You can download a trial version of SQL Server CE 1.1 on the Microsoft Web site (http://www.microsoft.com/sql/evaluation/trial/CE/download.asp). Additionally, you can find several good SQL Server CE articles and tutorials on the deVBuzz Web site (http://www.devbuzz.com/).

Summary

You now know more about programming a flexible Pocket Access application in eMbedded Visual Basic then you probably ever cared to know. Well, it only gets better. You're going to take everything you've learned up to this point to build the closest thing you can get to having the Microsoft Access 2000 design environment running on your Pocket PC.

CHAPTER 7

Pocket Access
Database Manager

YOU'VE FINALLY MADE IT TO the much-hyped chapter where I walk you through the construction of an application that enables you to manage your Pocket Access databases in a graphical manner. Whether you realize it or not, you already possess all the skills needed to accomplish this task as a result of your careful reading of Chapters 1 through 6. All you're going to do now is take a bunch of all too familiar code snippets and piece them together to build one program that combines all the DDL and DML statements you need to have complete control over your Pocket Access databases. Will this application be as powerful as Microsoft Access 2000? Probably not. Will it be as good as some of the Pocket Access database managers on the market that you have to pay for? Well, it will be better than some and almost as good as some others. The best part is that there's no limit to how far you can enhance and extend the code you're about to write. Think of what you're going to do here in Chapter 7 as building a code foundation that you take and make even better. Now prepare yourself, because 95 percent of what you'll read in this chapter is code and the other 5 percent is my commentary on and explanation of the code.

Getting Started

As I traversed through my own Envisioning and Planning Phases (a subtle plug for the Microsoft Solutions Framework), I wrestled with issues such as whether or not to spread the application out across multiple forms or to use a Tabstrip control on a single form. As you may or may not know, using multiple forms in eMbedded Visual Basic is a huge waste of memory because once you load a form in memory, it can't be unloaded until you shut down the application. You can only "show" and "hide" loaded forms, for some crazy reason. It is because of this limitation that you see so many single form applications that use multiple tabs instead of multiple forms. Slam dunk, right? Well, not so fast. I personally might build my applications that way, but describing this method of construction to a reader is by no means a simple task. I've instead decided to go with what I call the "single form, lots of menus, multiuse Grid method." Instead of just using the

Grid control to display data, you're going to use the Grid for everything imaginable. Your Grid will be used to display tables, data, and metadata.

Building the Form

In previous chapters, the graphical user interfaces of your applications have slowly taken shape over the course of the chapter. You didn't know for sure what the application was going to look like until you reached the end of the chapter and looked at a screen shot. It didn't really matter if your application looked like my application. In this chapter, it does matter. Therefore, I'm going to have you build out the look and feel of your Pocket Access Manager up front and then fill out the required code afterward. The look that you're after is shown in Figure 7-1.

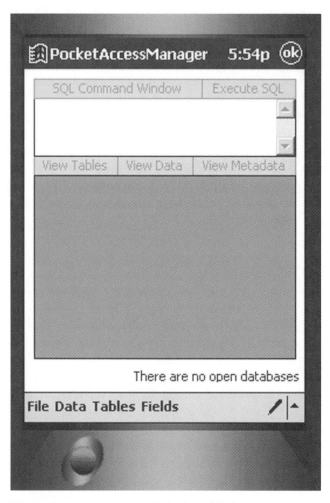

Figure 7-1. The Pocket Access Manager's look and feel

Let's start putting the pieces together. Bring up eMbedded Visual Basic, create a new Pocket PC project, and name it "PocketAccessManager." The default width of the main form, Form1, can be left alone, but stretch the height to 4605. Set the caption of Form1 to read "PocketAccessManager." Because this program is a database manager, set a reference to the Microsoft CE ADO Control 3.0. You'll need to add three components to the Toolbox, including the Microsoft CE Common Dialog Control 3.0, the Microsoft CE Grid Control 3.0, and the Microsoft Pocket PC Menubar Control 3.0. Drag the Grid control from the Toolbox and drop it on the form with the following properties:

- Top = 1320

- Left = 120

- Height = 2295

- Width = 3375

Now drag the Common Dialog and Menubar controls and drop them anywhere on the form—they work invisibly. All that remains now is to add seven intrinsic controls, so let's go from top to bottom. At the top left, add a CommandButton that you'll use as a label for the forthcoming SQL TextBox. Why not just use a Label control? Well, I thought that the CommandButton, with its grayed-out, disabled look, beat out the unimaginative label control. Set the following properties for the CommandButton:

- Top = 120

- Left = 120

- Height = 255

- Width = 2175

- Caption = "SQL Command Window"

- Enabled = "False"

At the top right, you need to add a CommandButton that will run the SQL statements in the upcoming SQL TextBox. Set the following properties for the CommandButton:

- Top = 120

- Left = 2280

- Height = 255

- Width = 1215

- Caption = "Execute SQL"

- Name = "cmdExecuteSQL"

Now, just below the two SQL CommandButtons, you will need to add a TextBox that will be used to enter SQL statements. Set the following properties for this TextBox:

- Top = 360

- Left = 120

- Height = 735

- Width = 3375

- Text = ""

- Name = "txtSQL"

Wedged between the SQL TextBox and the Grid will be a series of heavily used CommandButtons. The first CommandButton on the left will be called upon to display all the tables in the open database. Set the following properties for this CommandButton:

- Top = 1080

- Left = 120

- Height = 255

- Width = 1095

- Caption = "View Tables"

- Name = "cmdTableView"

The second CommandButton in this group will be used to display the data in the selected table. Set the following properties for this CommandButton:

- Top = 1080

- Left = 1200

- Height = 255

- Width = 975

- Caption = "View Data"

- Name = "cmdDataView"

The third CommandButton in this group will be used to display the Design view structure of a selected table. Set the following properties for this CommandButton:

- Top = 1080

- Left = 2169

- Height = 255

- Width = 1335

- Caption = "View Metadata"

- Name = "cmdMetaDataView"

The last thing you need to add to the form is a lowly Label control to display both the name and the state of the database. Set the following properties for this Label control:

- Top = 3720

- Left = 120

- Height = 180

- Width = 3420

- Caption = ""

- Name = "lblDBName"

Congratulations on successfully adding all the necessary GUI elements to the form! It's amazing that so few controls will end up doing so much work for you in this application. Now the easy part is over and it's time for you to start cranking out the code.

System-wide Variables

System performance is important and scalability isn't a concern because there's only one user. Therefore, you're going to use several global variables in this application. As a result of the fact that you're only using one form, there's no need to declare these variables in a Module. Because menus work differently in eMbedded Visual Basic than what you're used to on the desktop, you'll need to individually declare each of the four menus you'll use. Additionally, you'll need a persistent, global ADOCE Connection object. Finally, you'll need some helper variables to maintain state with various aspects of the database. In the General Declarations section of Form1, insert the following code:

```
Option Explicit

'Declare menus
Private FileMenu As MenuBarlib.MenuBarMenu
Private DataMenu As MenuBarlib.MenuBarMenu
Private TableMenu As MenuBarlib.MenuBarMenu
Private FieldMenu As MenuBarlib.MenuBarMenu
```

```
'Declare Connection object
Private CN As ADOCE.Connection

'Declare Globals
Private DatabasePath As String
Private DatabaseName As String
Private DatabaseState As Integer
Private CurrentTable As String
Private CurrentIndex As Long
```

Building the Menus

Just in case you thought I was kidding about menu differences, you're going to have to create a Sub that programmatically creates all the menus needed for the form. Even though Visual Basic developers have been complaining about the Visual Basic menu builder for years, it sure would be nice to have it around right about now. For each of the four menus, you have to manually add all the menu items, not to mention a separator bar here and there. Along with each item, you'll add a numeric index, a text-based key, and a menu caption. The indexes will be used to enable and disable the menu items when necessary. The keys will be used to determine which menu item was clicked. Create a Sub called "BuildMenus()" and add the following code:

```
Private Sub BuildMenus()

    'Create File Menu
    Set FileMenu = MenuBar1.Controls.AddMenu("File")
    FileMenu.Items.Add 1, "mnuCreateDatabase", "Create Database"
    FileMenu.Items.Add 2, "mnuDeleteDatabase", "Delete Database"
    FileMenu.Items.Add 3, "mnuSeparator1", ""
    FileMenu.Items(3).Style = mbrMenuSeparator
    FileMenu.Items.Add 4, "mnuOpenDatabase", "Open Database"
    FileMenu.Items.Add 5, "mnuCloseDatabase", "Close Database"
    FileMenu.Items.Add 6, "mnuSeparator2", ""
    FileMenu.Items(6).Style = mbrMenuSeparator
    FileMenu.Items.Add 7, "mnuExit", "Exit"

    'Create Data Menu
    Set DataMenu = MenuBar1.Controls.AddMenu("Data")
    DataMenu.Items.Add 1, "mnuAddData", "Add Data"
    DataMenu.Items.Add 2, "mnuUpdateData", "Update Selected Data"
```

```
DataMenu.Items.Add 3, "mnuDeleteData", "Delete Selected Data"
DataMenu.Items.Add 4, "mnuSortData", "Sort Selected Column"

'Create Table Menu
Set TableMenu = MenuBar1.Controls.AddMenu("Tables")
TableMenu.Items.Add 1, "mnuAddTable", "Add Table"
TableMenu.Items.Add 2, "mnuDeleteTable", "Delete Selected Table"
TableMenu.Items.Add 3, "mnuRenameTable", "Rename Selected Table"

'Create Fields Menu
Set FieldMenu = MenuBar1.Controls.AddMenu("Fields")
FieldMenu.Items.Add 1, "mnuAddField", "Add Field"
FieldMenu.Items.Add 2, "mnuDeleteField", "Delete Selected Field"
FieldMenu.Items.Add 3, "mnuRenameField", "Rename Selected Field"
FieldMenu.Items.Add 4, "mnuMoveFieldUp", "Move Selected Field Up"
FieldMenu.Items.Add 5, "mnuMoveFieldDown", "Move Selected Field Down"
FieldMenu.Items.Add 6, "mnuSeparator3", ""
FieldMenu.Items(6).Style = mbrMenuSeparator
FieldMenu.Items.Add 7, "mnuAddIndex", "Add Index"
FieldMenu.Items.Add 8, "mnuDeleteIndex", "Delete Selected Index"

End Sub
```

Reflecting Database State with Menus

Just as it's important to set a CommandButton's Enabled property to False to prevent a user from executing its code, so too will it be for your menu items. One of the global variables you created is used to keep track of whether a database is open or not. It's important to know this simple fact and have the menus react accordingly to prevent the user from causing preventable errors. If a database is closed, the user can choose to create a database, open a database, or exit the application. Likewise, if a database is open, the user can choose to delete the database, close the database, or exit the application. Menu items are enabled and disabled based on their index. Create a Sub called "ModifyMenus()" and add the following code:

```
Private Sub ModifyMenus()

    Select Case DatabaseState
        Case 0  'Database Closed
            'You can't delete a closed database
            FileMenu.Items(2).Enabled = False
```

```
            'You can't close a closed database
            FileMenu.Items(5).Enabled = False
            'You can create a new database
            FileMenu.Items(1).Enabled = True
            'You can open a database
            FileMenu.Items(4).Enabled = True

        Case 1  'Database Open
            'You can't create an open database
            FileMenu.Items(1).Enabled = False
            'You can't open an open database
            FileMenu.Items(4).Enabled = False
            'You can delete an open database
            FileMenu.Items(2).Enabled = True
            'You can close an open database
            FileMenu.Items(5).Enabled = True


        Case Else
    End Select


End Sub
```

Application Start-up

Now that you have a mechanism to build and manipulate menus, along with
some global variables thrown in for good measure, it's time to handle what happens when the application launches. There's nothing complicated here. You're
basically going to create the ADOCE Connection object for persistent use, set the
initial database state to Closed, construct the menus, and then modify the menus
based on the current state. Finally, you're going to notify the user that the database is closed through your Label control and then manually disable all the
CommandButtons and Menus to prevent the user from getting into trouble. In
the Form_Load event of your form, add the following code:

```
Private Sub Form_Load()

    'Instantiate the Connection Object
    Set CN = CreateObject("ADOCE.Connection.3.0")

    'Initial Database State is Closed
    DatabaseState = 0
```

```
        'Create Application Menus
        BuildMenus

        'Check Database State to ensure that the
        'proper menu items are enabled or disabled
        ModifyMenus

        'Display database status
        lblDBName = "There are no open databases"

        'Ensure that only relevant buttons and menus are visible
        cmdTableView.Enabled = False
        cmdDataView.Enabled = False
        cmdMetaDataView.Enabled = False
        cmdExecuteSQL.Enabled = False

        DataMenu.Items(1).Enabled = False      'Add Data
        DataMenu.Items(2).Enabled = False      'Update Selected Data
        DataMenu.Items(3).Enabled = False      'Delete Selected Data
        DataMenu.Items(4).Enabled = False      'Sort Selected Column

        TableMenu.Items(1).Enabled = False      'Add Table
        TableMenu.Items(2).Enabled = False      'Delete Selected Table
        TableMenu.Items(3).Enabled = False      'Rename Selected Table

        FieldMenu.Items(1).Enabled = False      'Add Field
        FieldMenu.Items(2).Enabled = False      'Delete Selected Field
        FieldMenu.Items(3).Enabled = False      'Rename Field
        FieldMenu.Items(4).Enabled = False      'Move Selected Field Up
        FieldMenu.Items(5).Enabled = False      'Move Selected Field Down
        FieldMenu.Items(7).Enabled = False      'Add Index
        FieldMenu.Items(8).Enabled = False      'Delete Selected Index


End Sub
```

Application Shutdown

By now you're accustomed to having the End method of the App object close your
eMbedded Visual Basic applications whenever the user clicks the OK button. That
method of closing an application isn't sufficient for your purposes here. To make
sure that your application closes in an orderly manner and cleans up after itself,
you'll need to add code to ensure that ADOCE Recordset and Connection objects

get closed and dereferenced. Your Pocket Access databases will thank you for this. Create a Sub called "Shutdown()" and add the following code:

```
Private Sub Shutdown()

    On Error Resume Next

    'Close the Recordset
    If RS.State = 1 Then
        RS.Close
    End If

    'Close the database
    If CN.State = 1 Then
        CN.Close
    End If

    'Dereference the Recordset
    Set RS = Nothing

    'Dereference the Connection
    Set CN = Nothing

    App.End

End Sub
```

Responding to Menu Clicks

With your application up and running, you're going to have all kinds of menu items that will perform the majority of the tasks. In Visual Basic 6.0, each menu item has its own click event, which makes for easy coding. With eMbedded Visual Basic, you only get a single menu click event to handle everything. Luckily, the event passes in the Item object of the Menubar control so that you can grab hold of all the keys. You'll use a Case statement with all possible menu item keys listed to call the appropriate Subs when an item is clicked. In the MenuBar1_MenuClick event, add the following code:

```
Private Sub MenuBar1_MenuClick(ByVal Item As MenuBarlib.Item)

    Select Case Item.Key
```

```
            Case "mnuCreateDatabase"
                'Create a new database
                CreateDatabase

            Case "mnuDeleteDatabase"
                'Delete the opened database
                DeleteDatabase

            Case "mnuOpenDatabase"
                'Open an existing database
                OpenDatabase

            Case "mnuCloseDatabase"
                'Close an opened database
                CloseDatabase

            Case "mnuExit"
                'Close Application
                Shutdown

            Case "mnuAddData"
                'Add Data
                AddData

            Case "mnuUpdateData"
                'Update Selected Data
                UpdateSelectedData

            Case "mnuDeleteData"
                'Delete Selected Data
                DeleteSelectedData

            Case "mnuAddTable"
                'Add a Table
                AddTable

            Case "mnuDeleteTable"
                'Delete Selected Table
                DeleteSelectedTable

            Case "mnuRenameTable"
                'Rename the selected table
                RenameSelectedTable
```

```
        Case "mnuAddField"
            'Add a new field to a table
            AddField

        Case "mnuDeleteField"
            'Delete the selected field
            DeleteSelectedField

        Case "mnuRenameField"
            'Rename the selected field
            RenameSelectedField

        Case "mnuMoveFieldUp"
            'Move the selected field up
            MoveSelectedFieldUp

        Case "mnuMoveFieldDown"
            'Move the selected field down
            MoveSelectedFieldDown

        Case "mnuAddIndex"
            'Add an Index
            AddSelectedIndex

        Case "mnuDeleteIndex"
            'Delete an Index
            DeleteSelectedIndex

        Case "mnuSortData"
            'Sort selected column
            SortData


    Case Else

    End Select

End Sub
```

Working with Databases

In this application, you're going to do four basic things with Pocket Access databases: You're going to open them, close them, create them, and delete them using the DDL skills you picked up in Chapter 2 so that you end up with something that looks like Figure 7-2.

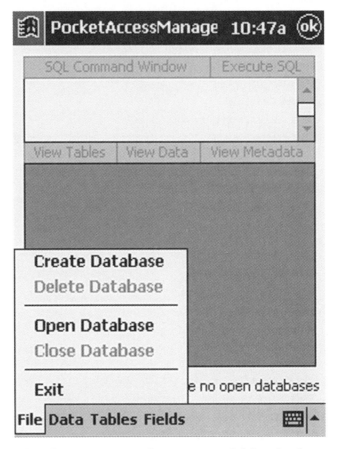

Figure 7-2. The File menu to open, close, create, and delete databases

Creating a Database

For a user to construct a new database, all he or she needs to do is select Create Database from the File menu. One of the simplest things you can do with ADOCE is create a database. All you need is a database name, a path, and the CREATE DATABASE statement. In this section, you'll use an InputBox to capture the desired database name and you'll create that database in the My Documents folder. The database name and path will be maintained throughout the life of the application in the DatabasePath variable. Once the database has been successfully created, you'll open it with the Connection object, you'll change the database state to Open, you'll modify the file menus, and your label will tell the user that the database is now open for business. You'll then go about using your multiuse Grid control to display any user-created tables that exist in the database. Obviously, there won't be any tables listed in the Grid because you just created the database. Finally, you'll enable all the Table menu items as well as all the CommandButtons to let the user know that they're available for use. Oh, and if things don't work out, you'll display an error message and let the user try again. Create a Sub called "CreateDatabase()" and add the following code:

```
Private Sub CreateDatabase()

    On Error Resume Next

    'Get the name of the new database
    DatabaseName = InputBox("Enter a name for your new database",
                            "Create Database")

    If DatabaseName <> "" Then

        'Put together the database path
        DatabasePath = "\My Documents\" & DatabaseName & ".cdb"

        'Create Recordset Object
        Dim RS As ADOCE.Recordset
        Set RS = CreateObject("ADOCE.Recordset.3.0")

        'Create the Database
        RS.Open "CREATE DATABASE '" & DatabasePath & "'"

        If Err.Number = 0 Then

            MsgBox "Your database, '" & DatabaseName &
            "' has been sucessfully created in the 'My Documents' folder."

            'Open the database
            CN.Open DatabasePath

            'Database state is now open
            DatabaseState = 1

            'Modify menus to reflect new database state
            ModifyMenus
```

```
lblDBName = DatabaseName & " is open"

'Remove existing data from Grid
GridCtrl1.Redraw = False
For i = 1 To GridCtrl1.Rows
    GridCtrl1.RemoveItem 0
Next

GridCtrl1.Cols = 2
GridCtrl1.ColWidth(0) = 110 * Len("Table Name")
GridCtrl1.ColWidth(1) = 110 * Len("Table ID")

GridCtrl1.AddItem "Table Name" & vbTab & "Table ID"

'Display Tables
RS.Open "MSysTables", CN
While Not RS.EOF

    'Disregard all System Tables
    If RS("TableName") <> "MSysTables" _
    And RS("TableName") <> "MSysIndexes" _
    And RS("TableName") <> "MSysFields" _
    And RS("TableName") <> "MSysProcs" Then
        'Add table to combo box
        GridCtrl1.AddItem RS("TableName") & vbTab & RS("TableID")
    End If

    RS.MoveNext
Wend

GridCtrl1.Redraw = True

RS.Close

cmdTableView.Enabled = True
cmdDataView.Enabled = True
cmdMetaDataView.Enabled = True
cmdExecuteSQL.Enabled = True

TableMenu.Items(1).Enabled = True    'Add Table
TableMenu.Items(2).Enabled = True    'Delete Selected Table
TableMenu.Items(3).Enabled = True    'Rename Selected Table

Else
```

```
                'Display database creation error
                MsgBox Err.Description
                'Database state remains closed
                DatabaseState = 0
                'Zero-out the database name and path
                DatabaseName = ""
                DatabasePath = ""

        End If

        Set RS = Nothing

    End If

End Sub
```

Opening a Database

A user opens a database when he or she selects Open Database from the File menu. In order to open a database, you must first piece together the database name and path. The easiest way to accomplish this task is to use the Common Dialog control to let the user navigate to the desired file. In this case, your Common Dialog box will make it easy by displaying any file on your Pocket PC that ends in .cdb. The global DatabasePath variable will maintain the path that the user selects throughout the life of the application. You'll then open the selected database with the Connection object, parse the database name from the DatabasePath variable, and display it in the label. Along the way, you'll set the database state to Open, modify the File menus, display all the user-created tables in the Grid, and enable all the CommandButtons and the Table menu items. Create a Sub called "OpenDatabase()" and add the following code:

```
Private Sub OpenDatabase()

    On Error Resume Next

    Dim fileflags As FileOpenConstants
    Dim e As Variant
    Dim i As Integer

    'Set the text in the dialog box title bar
    CommonDialog1.DialogTitle = "Open Database"
```

```
'Set the default filename and filter
CommonDialog1.InitDir = "\"
CommonDialog1.FileName = ""
CommonDialog1.Filter = "Pocket Access (*.cdb)|*.cdb"

'Verify that the file exists
CommonDialog1.Flags = cdlOFNFileMustExist

'Show the Open common dialog box
CommonDialog1.ShowOpen

'Return the path and filename selected or
'Return an empty string if the user cancels the dialog box
DatabasePath = CommonDialog1.FileName

If DatabasePath <> "" Then

    'Open the database
    CN.Open DatabasePath

    'Display Connection Errors
    For Each e In CN.Errors
        MsgBox e.Description
    Next

    Dim Position As Integer

    Position = InStrRev(DatabasePath, "\")
    DatabaseName = Right(DatabasePath, Len(DatabasePath) - Position)

    'Database state is now open
    DatabaseState = 1
    'Modify menus to reflect new database state
    ModifyMenus

    lblDBName = DatabaseName & " is open"

    'Remove existing data from Grid
    GridCtrl1.Redraw = False
    For i = 1 To GridCtrl1.Rows
        GridCtrl1.RemoveItem 0
    Next

    GridCtrl1.Cols = 2
```

```
    GridCtrl1.ColWidth(0) = 110 * Len("Table Name")
    GridCtrl1.ColWidth(1) = 110 * Len("Table ID")


    GridCtrl1.AddItem "Table Name" & vbTab & "Table ID"

    'Create Recordset Object
    Dim RS As ADOCE.Recordset
    Set RS = CreateObject("ADOCE.Recordset.3.0")

    'Display Tables
    RS.Open "MSysTables", CN
    While Not RS.EOF

        'Disregard all System Tables
        If RS("TableName") <> "MSysTables" _
        And RS("TableName") <> "MSysIndexes" _
        And RS("TableName") <> "MSysFields" _
        And RS("TableName") <> "MSysProcs" Then
            'Add table to combo box
            GridCtrl1.AddItem RS("TableName") & vbTab & RS("TableID")
        End If

        RS.MoveNext
    Wend

    GridCtrl1.Redraw = True

    RS.Close

    cmdTableView.Enabled = True
    cmdDataView.Enabled = True
    cmdMetaDataView.Enabled = True
    cmdExecuteSQL.Enabled = True

    TableMenu.Items(1).Enabled = True    'Add Table
    TableMenu.Items(2).Enabled = True    'Delete Selected Table
    TableMenu.Items(3).Enabled = True    'Rename Selected Table

    Set RS = Nothing

    End If

End Sub
```

Closing a Database

Selecting Close Database from the File menu is all it takes to close a database. The code to close a database is the same as the code you used in the Shutdown Sub. If a database is open, then close it. After that, you do something interesting. Remember that global, persistent Connection object? Once you close the database, you set the Connection object equal to nothing and then you re-create it. Why? Until you dereference the Connection object, you still have an open handle connected to that database that prevents you from completely closing it. Once the database is truly closed, you'll clear out the Grid, set the database state to Closed, modify the File menus, and tell the user that the database is closed. Finally, you'll disable every CommandButton and menu. Create a Sub called "CloseDatabase()" and add the following code:

```
Private Sub CloseDatabase()

    On Error Resume Next

    Dim i

    'Close the database
    If CN.State = 1 Then
        CN.Close
    End If

    'Dereference the Connection
    Set CN = Nothing

    'Reinstantiate the Connection Object
    Set CN = CreateObject("ADOCE.Connection.3.0")

    'Remove existing data from Grid
    GridCtrl1.Redraw = False
    For i = 1 To GridCtrl1.Rows
        GridCtrl1.RemoveItem 0
    Next
    GridCtrl1.Redraw = True

    'Database state is closed
    DatabaseState = 0
    'Modify menus to reflect new database state
    ModifyMenus
    'Zero-out the database name and path
```

```
    DatabaseName = ""
    DatabasePath = ""

    lblDBName = "There are no open databases"

    cmdTableView.Enabled = False
    cmdDataView.Enabled = False
    cmdMetaDataView.Enabled = False
    cmdExecuteSQL.Enabled = False

    DataMenu.Items(1).Enabled = False    'Add Data
    DataMenu.Items(2).Enabled = False    'Update Selected Data
    DataMenu.Items(3).Enabled = False    'Delete Selected Data
    DataMenu.Items(4).Enabled = False    'Sort Selected Column

    TableMenu.Items(1).Enabled = False    'Add Table
    TableMenu.Items(2).Enabled = False    'Delete Selected Table
    TableMenu.Items(3).Enabled = False    'Rename Selected Table

    FieldMenu.Items(1).Enabled = False    'Add Field
    FieldMenu.Items(2).Enabled = False    'Delete Selected Field
    FieldMenu.Items(3).Enabled = False    'Rename Field
    FieldMenu.Items(4).Enabled = False    'Move Selected Field Up
    FieldMenu.Items(5).Enabled = False    'Move Selected Field Down
    FieldMenu.Items(7).Enabled = False    'Add Index
    FieldMenu.Items(8).Enabled = False    'Delete Selected Index


End Sub
```

Deleting a Database

You can only delete a database that's currently open in this application. Doing so requires that you select Delete Database from the File menu. The code to delete a database is identical to the code used to close a database, with one exception. You'll create and use a Recordset object to execute the DROP DATABASE statement to effectively delete the open database. Create a Sub called "DeleteDatabase()" and add the following code:

```
Private Sub DeleteDatabase()

    On Error Resume Next

    Dim i

    'Close the database
    If CN.State = 1 Then
        CN.Close
    End If

    'Dereference the Connection
    Set CN = Nothing

    'Create Recordset Object
    Dim RS As ADOCE.Recordset
    Set RS = CreateObject("ADOCE.Recordset.3.0")

    'Delete the Database
    RS.Open "DROP DATABASE '" & DatabasePath & "'"

    'Reinstantiate the Connection Object
    Set CN = CreateObject("ADOCE.Connection.3.0")

    'Remove existing data from Grid
    GridCtrl1.Redraw = False
    For i = 1 To GridCtrl1.Rows
        GridCtrl1.RemoveItem 0
    Next
    GridCtrl1.Redraw = True

    'Database state is closed
    DatabaseState = 0
    'Modify menus to reflect new database state
```

```
    ModifyMenus
    'Zero-out the database name and path
    DatabaseName = ""
    DatabasePath = ""

    lblDBName = "There are no open databases"

    cmdTableView.Enabled = False
    cmdDataView.Enabled = False
    cmdMetaDataView.Enabled = False
    cmdExecuteSQL.Enabled = False

    DataMenu.Items(1).Enabled = False     'Add Data
    DataMenu.Items(2).Enabled = False     'Update Selected Data
    DataMenu.Items(3).Enabled = False     'Delete Selected Data
    DataMenu.Items(4).Enabled = False     'Sort Selected Column

    TableMenu.Items(1).Enabled = False    'Add Table
    TableMenu.Items(2).Enabled = False    'Delete Selected Table
    TableMenu.Items(3).Enabled = False    'Rename Selected Table

    FieldMenu.Items(1).Enabled = False    'Add Field
    FieldMenu.Items(2).Enabled = False    'Delete Selected Field
    FieldMenu.Items(3).Enabled = False    'Rename Field
    FieldMenu.Items(4).Enabled = False    'Move Selected Field Up
    FieldMenu.Items(5).Enabled = False    'Move Selected Field Down
    FieldMenu.Items(7).Enabled = False    'Add Index
    FieldMenu.Items(8).Enabled = False    'Delete Selected Index

    Set RS = Nothing

End Sub
```

Working with Tables

You'll add, delete, rename, and display tables in the Grid with the help of your Tables menu, as shown in Figure 7-3.

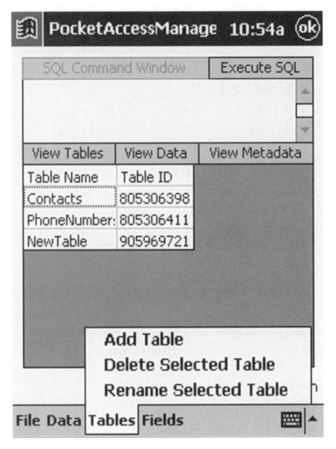

Figure 7-3. The Tables menu

Viewing Tables

A user who wants to view all the tables in a database must click the View Tables button to do so. The application's ability to display tables has already been demonstrated in both the OpenDatabase and CreateDatabase Subs. Here you're just going to add two columns to the Grid to display the TableName and the TableID. The TableID may appear to be useless fluff to the average user, but knowing that ID is the only way to determine the existence of an indexed field in any given table. The user can view the tables in a database by clicking the View

Tables button. At the end, you ensure that only the CommandButtons and the
Table menu items are available for selection by the user. Create a Sub called
"ViewTables()" and add the following code:

```
Private Sub ViewTables()

    On Error Resume Next

    Dim i As Integer

    'Remove existing data from Grid
    GridCtrl1.Redraw = False
    For i = 1 To GridCtrl1.Rows
        GridCtrl1.RemoveItem 0
    Next

    GridCtrl1.Cols = 2

    GridCtrl1.ColWidth(0) = 110 * Len("Table Name")
    GridCtrl1.ColWidth(1) = 110 * Len("Table ID")

    GridCtrl1.AddItem "Table Name" & vbTab & "Table ID"

    'Create Recordset Object
    Dim RS As ADOCE.Recordset
    Set RS = CreateObject("ADOCE.Recordset.3.0")

    'Display Tables
    RS.Open "MSysTables", CN
    While Not RS.EOF

        'Disregard all System Tables
        If RS("TableName") <> "MSysTables" _
        And RS("TableName") <> "MSysIndexes" _
        And RS("TableName") <> "MSysFields" _
        And RS("TableName") <> "MSysProcs" Then
            'Add table to combo box
            GridCtrl1.AddItem RS("TableName") & vbTab & RS("TableID")
        End If
```

```
        RS.MoveNext
Wend

GridCtrl1.Redraw = True

RS.Close

cmdDataView.Enabled = True
cmdMetaDataView.Enabled = True
cmdExecuteSQL.Enabled = True

DataMenu.Items(1).Enabled = False    'Add Data
DataMenu.Items(2).Enabled = False    'Update Selected Data
DataMenu.Items(3).Enabled = False    'Delete Selected Data
DataMenu.Items(4).Enabled = False    'Sort Selected Column

TableMenu.Items(1).Enabled = True    'Add Table
TableMenu.Items(2).Enabled = True    'Delete Selected Table
TableMenu.Items(3).Enabled = True    'Rename Selected Table

FieldMenu.Items(1).Enabled = False    'Add Field
FieldMenu.Items(2).Enabled = False    'Delete Selected Field
FieldMenu.Items(3).Enabled = False    'Rename Field
FieldMenu.Items(4).Enabled = False    'Move Selected Field Up
FieldMenu.Items(5).Enabled = False    'Move Selected Field Down
FieldMenu.Items(7).Enabled = False    'Add Index
FieldMenu.Items(8).Enabled = False    'Delete Selected Index

Set RS = Nothing

End Sub
```

Adding a Table

You might think that adding a new table to the database only requires a table name and a call to the CREATE TABLE statement. Unfortunately, you have to create at least one field in the new table in order to make the thing work. Everything gets started when the user selects the Add Table menu item. The first thing you'll do is use an InputBox to capture a table name from the user. Next, you'll use another InputBox to capture the name of the field you need to create. Finally, you'll use yet another InputBox to retrieve the desired data type for this new field in this new table. Now you'll use a Case statement based on the entered data type to create the table and field. The reason you use a Case statement is to throw out any mistyped data types and to detect if the user chose a varchar or varbinary data type. These two data types require a length parameter that will be retrieved using another InputBox. Once all the data is captured and the table is created, you run through the familiar code used to display tables in the Grid. Create a Sub called "AddTable()" and add the following code:

```
Private Sub AddTable()

    On Error Resume Next

    Dim TableName As String
    Dim FieldName As String
    Dim DataType As String
    Dim DataLength As Integer
    Dim i As Integer

    'Get the name of the new table
    TableName = InputBox("Enter a name for your new Table", "Create Table")

    'Get the name of the new field
    FieldName = InputBox("You must create at least one field in this new table,
    so please enter a name for this new field.", "Create Table")

    'Get the Data Type of the new field
    DataType = InputBox("Enter one of the following data types: Varchar, Text,
     Varbinary, Long Varbinary, Int, SmallInt, Float, DateTime, Bit.",
     "Create Table")

    'Create Recordset Object
    Dim RS As ADOCE.Recordset
    Set RS = CreateObject("ADOCE.Recordset.3.0")
```

```
'Validate user input
Select Case LCase(DataType)
    Case "varchar"
        DataLength = CInt(InputBox("Enter the length of your
                        Varchar field from 1 to 255.", "Create Table"))
        If DataLength > 0 And DataLength < 256 Then
            RS.Open "CREATE TABLE " & TableName & " (" & FieldName &
                        " Varchar(" & DataLength & "))", CN
        End If

    Case "text"
        RS.Open "CREATE TABLE " & TableName & " (" & FieldName & " Text)", CN

    Case "varbinary"
        DataLength = CInt(InputBox("Enter the length of your Varbinary field
                        from 1 to 255.", "Create Table"))
        If DataLength > 0 And DataLength < 256 Then
            RS.Open "CREATE TABLE " & TableName & " (" & FieldName &
                        " Varbinary(" & DataLength & "))", CN
        End If

    Case "long varbinary"
        RS.Open "CREATE TABLE " & TableName & " (" & FieldName &
                    " Long Varbinary)", CN

    Case "int"
        RS.Open "CREATE TABLE " & TableName & " (" & FieldName & " Int)", CN

    Case "smallint"
        RS.Open "CREATE TABLE " & TableName & " (" & FieldName & " Smallint)"
                    , CN

    Case "float"
        RS.Open "CREATE TABLE " & TableName & " (" & FieldName & " Float)", CN

    Case "datetime"
        RS.Open "CREATE TABLE " & TableName & " (" &
                    FieldName & " Datetime)", CN

    Case "bit"
        RS.Open "CREATE TABLE " & TableName & " (" & FieldName & " Bit)", CN
```

```
        Case Else
            MsgBox "Unrecognized Data Type, please try this operation again."
            Exit Sub

    End Select

    'Remove existing data from Grid
    GridCtrl1.Redraw = False
    For i = 1 To GridCtrl1.Rows
        GridCtrl1.RemoveItem 0
    Next

    GridCtrl1.Cols = 2
    GridCtrl1.ColWidth(0) = 110 * Len("Table Name")
    GridCtrl1.ColWidth(1) = 110 * Len("Table ID")

    GridCtrl1.AddItem "Table Name" & vbTab & "Table ID"

    'Display Tables
    RS.Open "MSysTables", CN
    While Not RS.EOF

        'Disregard all System Tables
        If RS("TableName") <> "MSysTables" _
        And RS("TableName") <> "MSysIndexes" _
        And RS("TableName") <> "MSysFields" _
        And RS("TableName") <> "MSysProcs" Then
            'Add table to combo box
            GridCtrl1.AddItem RS("TableName") & vbTab & RS("TableID")
        End If

        RS.MoveNext
    Wend

    GridCtrl1.Redraw = True

    RS.Close
    Set RS = Nothing

End Sub
```

Renaming a Table

Renaming a table is a straightforward and simple matter. Basically, you have the user click the table they want to rename on the Grid. That action enables you to capture the current table name once the user has selected the Rename Selected Table menu item. You then prompt the user for the new table name using an InputBox. Once you call the ALTER TABLE statement, you'll clear out the Grid and refill it to reflect the changed table name. Create a Sub called "RenameSelectedTable()" and add the following code:

```
Private Sub RenameSelectedTable()

    On Error Resume Next

    Dim NewTable As String

    'Ensure that the following code is executed
    'only if the user clicks a valid nonheader row.
    If GridCtrl1.RowSel > 0 Then

        NewTable = InputBox("Enter a new Table Name", "Rename Table")

        'Create Recordset Object
        Dim RS As ADOCE.Recordset
        Set RS = CreateObject("ADOCE.Recordset.3.0")

        If NewTable <> "" Then
            RS.Open "ALTER TABLE " & GridCtrl1.TextMatrix(GridCtrl1.RowSel, 0) &
                        " TO " & NewTable, CN
        Else
            MsgBox "You must enter a new table name.
                        Please try this operation again."
            Exit Sub
        End If

        Dim i As Integer

        'Remove existing data from Grid
        GridCtrl1.Redraw = False
        For i = 1 To GridCtrl1.Rows
            GridCtrl1.RemoveItem 0
        Next
```

```
GridCtrl1.Cols = 2
GridCtrl1.ColWidth(0) = 110 * Len("Table Name")
GridCtrl1.ColWidth(1) = 110 * Len("Table ID")

GridCtrl1.AddItem "Table Name" & vbTab & "Table ID"

'Display Tables
RS.Open "MSysTables", CN
While Not RS.EOF

    'Disregard all System Tables
    If RS("TableName") <> "MSysTables" _
    And RS("TableName") <> "MSysIndexes" _
    And RS("TableName") <> "MSysFields" _
    And RS("TableName") <> "MSysProcs" Then
        'Add table to combo box
        GridCtrl1.AddItem RS("TableName") & vbTab & RS("TableID")
    End If

    RS.MoveNext
Wend

GridCtrl1.Redraw = True

RS.Close

Set RS = Nothing

End If

End Sub
```

Deleting a Table

Deleting a table is even easier than renaming a table. The code gets kicked off when the user selects the Delete Selected Table menu item. You capture the table to delete when the user clicks the desired table in the Grid. After that, it's just a matter of calling the DROP TABLE statement and refreshing the Grid so that the user sees that it's gone. Create a Sub called "DeleteSelectedTable()" and add the following code:

```
Private Sub DeleteSelectedTable()

    On Error Resume Next

    Dim i As Integer

    'Ensure that the following code is executed
    'only if the user clicks a valid nonheader row.
    If GridCtrl1.RowSel > 0 Then

        'Create Recordset Object
        Dim RS As ADOCE.Recordset
        Set RS = CreateObject("ADOCE.Recordset.3.0")

        RS.Open "DROP TABLE " & GridCtrl1.TextMatrix(GridCtrl1.RowSel, 0), CN

        'Remove existing data from Grid
        GridCtrl1.Redraw = False
        For i = 1 To GridCtrl1.Rows
            GridCtrl1.RemoveItem 0
        Next

        GridCtrl1.Cols = 2
        GridCtrl1.ColWidth(0) = 110 * Len("Table Name")
        GridCtrl1.ColWidth(1) = 110 * Len("Table ID")

        GridCtrl1.AddItem "Table Name" & vbTab & "Table ID"
```

```
'Display Tables
RS.Open "MSysTables", CN
While Not RS.EOF

    'Disregard all System Tables
    If RS("TableName") <> "MSysTables" _
    And RS("TableName") <> "MSysIndexes" _
    And RS("TableName") <> "MSysFields" _
    And RS("TableName") <> "MSysProcs" Then
        'Add table to combo box
        GridCtrl1.AddItem RS("TableName") & vbTab & RS("TableID")
    End If

    RS.MoveNext
Wend

GridCtrl1.Redraw = True

RS.Close

Set RS = Nothing

    End If

End Sub
```

Working with Fields

You'll add, delete, rename, move, and display field metadata in the Grid with the help of the Fields menu, as shown in Figure 7-4.

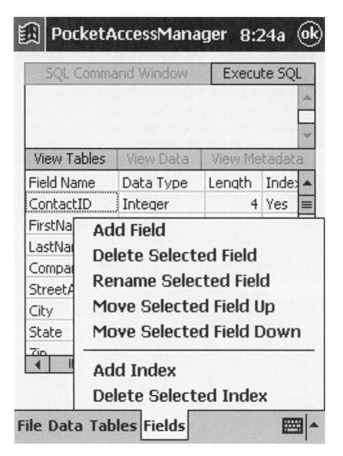

Figure 7-4. The Fields menu

Viewing Fields

The fields within a table are made available for viewing whenever the user selects
a table in the Grid and then clicks the View Metadata button. The very first thing that
happens is that you don't execute any code unless the user has selected
a nonheader cell in the Grid. You then capture the TableName as well as
the TableID so that you'll be equipped with everything you need to display the
metadata. You also store the TableID in the global CurrentIndex variable for
instances where you'll need that information in the future without the need
for clicking the Grid to recapture that information. Moving right along, you loop
through the MSysIndexes system table looking for a match for your TableID so that
you're only looking at the indexes for the table you care about. You then find the
name of the index for that table and the FieldID that gives you your first clue as to
which field in the table is indexed. Next, you loop through the MSysFields system
table searching for the FieldID and TableID that match your FieldID and TableID

variables. Once you've found the match, you set that FieldName equal to your IndexedFieldName variable for use later on. Now it's time to display the field names, data types, data type length, indexed field, and index name in your Grid. After clearing the Grid and populating the column headers, you start to iterate through the Fields Collection of your table's Recordset. Each time you loop through the Fields Collection, you run the field's Type through a Case statement in order to display meaningful data type names instead of numbers. After that, you grab both the field's name and its length. Finally, you check and see if that field happens to be the indexed field by comparing it with your IndexedFieldName variable. With all the information gathered, you add the row to the Grid and then start another iteration. For a finishing touch, make sure that all but the Execute SQL buttons are disabled and only the Fields menu items are enabled. Create a Sub called "ViewMetaData()" and add the following code:

```
Private Sub ViewMetaData()

    On Error Resume Next

    Dim i As Integer
    Dim FieldType As String
    Dim FieldName As String
    Dim IndexName As String
    Dim FieldID As Integer
    Dim TableID As Long
    Dim IndexedFieldName As String
    Dim Indexed As String
    Dim FieldLength As Integer

    'Ensure that the following code is executed
    'only if the user clicks a valid nonheader row.
    If GridCtrl1.RowSel > 0 Then

        CurrentTable = GridCtrl1.TextMatrix(GridCtrl1.RowSel, 0)
        CurrentIndex = CLng(GridCtrl1.TextMatrix(GridCtrl1.RowSel, 1))

        TableID = CLng(GridCtrl1.TextMatrix(GridCtrl1.RowSel, 1))

        Dim RSFields As ADOCE.Recordset
        Set RSFields = CreateObject("ADOCE.Recordset.3.0")

        'Create Recordset Object
        Dim RS As ADOCE.Recordset
        Set RS = CreateObject("ADOCE.Recordset.3.0")

        'View all Indexes
```

```
RS.Open "MSysIndexes", CN
While Not RS.EOF

    'Only look at Indexes in the current table
    If (TableID = CLng(RS("TableID"))) Then

        IndexName = RS("IndexName")
        FieldID = RS("FieldID")

        RSFields.Open "MSysFields", CN
        While Not RSFields.EOF

            If RSFields("FieldID") = FieldID And
               RSFields("TableID") = TableID Then
                 IndexedFieldName = RSFields("FieldName")

            End If
            RSFields.MoveNext
        Wend
        RSFields.Close

    End If

    RS.MoveNext
Wend
RS.Close

Set RSFields = Nothing

'A keyset-based, forward and backward, read and write Recordset
RS.Open GridCtrl1.TextMatrix(GridCtrl1.RowSel, 0), CN

'Remove existing data from Grid
GridCtrl1.Redraw = False
For i = 1 To GridCtrl1.Rows
    GridCtrl1.RemoveItem 0
Next

GridCtrl1.Cols = 5
GridCtrl1.ColWidth(0) = 110 * Len("Field Name")
GridCtrl1.ColWidth(1) = 110 * Len("Data Type")
GridCtrl1.ColWidth(2) = 110 * Len("Length")
GridCtrl1.ColWidth(3) = 110 * Len("Indexed")
```

```
GridCtrl1.ColWidth(4) = 110 * Len("Index Name")

GridCtrl1.AddItem "Field Name" & vbTab & "Data Type" & vbTab & "Length" &
                        vbTab & "Indexed" & vbTab & "Index Name"


'View Fields
For i = 0 To RS.Fields.Count - 1

    'Convert the Field Type number
    'into a meaningful string
    Select Case RS.Fields(i).Type
        Case 202
            FieldType = "Varchar"
        Case 203
            FieldType = "Text"
        Case 204
            FieldType = "Varbinary"
        Case 205
            FieldType = "Long Varbinary"
        Case 3
            FieldType = "Integer"
        Case 2
            FieldType = "Smallint"
        Case 5
            FieldType = "Float"
        Case 7
            FieldType = "Datetime"
        Case 11
            FieldType = "Bit"
    End Select

    'Get the Field Name
    FieldName = RS.Fields(i).Name

    'Get the Field Length
    FieldLength = RS.Fields(i).DefinedSize

    If FieldName = IndexedFieldName Then
        GridCtrl1.AddItem FieldName & vbTab & FieldType & vbTab &
        FieldLength & vbTab & "Yes" & vbTab & IndexName
    Else
        GridCtrl1.AddItem FieldName & vbTab & FieldType & vbTab &
        FieldLength & vbTab & "No" & vbTab & ""
    End If
```

```
            Next
            RS.Close

            GridCtrl1.Redraw = True

            cmdDataView.Enabled = False
            cmdMetaDataView.Enabled = False
            cmdExecuteSQL.Enabled = True

            DataMenu.Items(1).Enabled = False    'Add Data
            DataMenu.Items(2).Enabled = False    'Update Selected Data
            DataMenu.Items(3).Enabled = False    'Delete Selected Data
            DataMenu.Items(4).Enabled = False    'Sort Selected Column

            TableMenu.Items(1).Enabled = False    'Add Table
            TableMenu.Items(2).Enabled = False    'Delete Selected Table
            TableMenu.Items(3).Enabled = False    'Rename Selected Table

            FieldMenu.Items(1).Enabled = True    'Add Field
            FieldMenu.Items(2).Enabled = True    'Delete Selected Field
            FieldMenu.Items(3).Enabled = True    'Rename Field
            FieldMenu.Items(4).Enabled = True    'Move Selected Field Up
            FieldMenu.Items(5).Enabled = True    'Move Selected Field Down
            FieldMenu.Items(7).Enabled = True    'Add Index
            FieldMenu.Items(8).Enabled = True    'Delete Selected Index

            Set RS = Nothing

        End If

End Sub
```

The results of this Sub should look something like Figure 7-5.

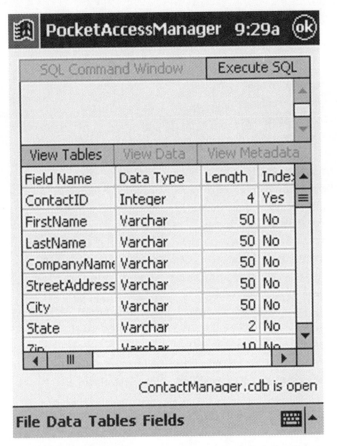

Figure 7-5. Metadata display

Adding a Field

The process of adding a field begins when the user selects the Add Field menu item. What happens next is somewhat similar to the extra steps that created a single field when adding a table. First of all, the user is prompted to enter the name of the new field with an InputBox. An InputBox is then used again to enable the user to enter the data type for this new field. You then run through a familiar Case statement based on the data type that was entered. As you may remember, if the user selected a varchar or varbinary data type, the user will be prompted for the length of that data type with an InputBox. The field is then added using the ALTER TABLE statement with the ADD parameter. Once the field is added, you refresh the Grid and run through the same code used in the ViewMetaData Sub. Create a Sub called "AddField()" and add the following code:

```
Private Sub AddField()

    On Error Resume Next

    Dim FieldName As String
    Dim DataType As String
    Dim DataLength As Integer
    Dim i As Integer
    Dim FieldType As String
    Dim IndexName As String
    Dim FieldID As Integer
    Dim TableID As Long
    Dim IndexedFieldName As String
    Dim Indexed As String
    Dim FieldLength As Integer

    'Get the name of the new table
    FieldName = InputBox("Enter a name for your new Field", "Create Field")

    'Get the Data Type of the new field
    DataType = InputBox("Enter one of the following data types: Varchar, Text,
Varbinary, Long Varbinary, Int, SmallInt, Float, DateTime, Bit.", "Create Table")

    If FieldName <> "" And DataType <> "" Then

        'Create Recordset Object
        Dim RS As ADOCE.Recordset
        Set RS = CreateObject("ADOCE.Recordset.3.0")

        'Validate user input
        Select Case LCase(DataType)
            Case "varchar"
                DataLength = CInt(InputBox("Enter the length of your Varchar
                                    field from 1 to 255.", "Create Field"))
                If DataLength > 0 And DataLength < 256 Then
                    RS.Open "ALTER TABLE " & CurrentTable & " ADD " & FieldName &
                                    " Varchar(" & DataLength & ")", CN
                End If

            Case "text"
                RS.Open "ALTER TABLE " & CurrentTable & " ADD " & FieldName &
                                "Text ", CN
```

```
    Case "varbinary"
        DataLength = CInt(InputBox("Enter the length of your Varbinary
                          field from 1 to 255.", "Create Field"))
        If DataLength > 0 And DataLength < 256 Then
            RS.Open "ALTER TABLE " & CurrentTable & " ADD " & FieldName &
                          " Varbinary(" & DataLength & ")", CN
        End If

    Case "long varbinary"
        RS.Open "ALTER TABLE " & CurrentTable & " ADD " & FieldName &
                      " Long Varbinary", CN

    Case "int"
        RS.Open "ALTER TABLE " & CurrentTable & " ADD " & FieldName &
                      " Int", CN

    Case "smallint"
        RS.Open "ALTER TABLE " & CurrentTable & " ADD " & FieldName &
                      " Smallint", CN

    Case "float"
        RS.Open "ALTER TABLE " & CurrentTable & " ADD " & FieldName &
                      " Float", CN

    Case "datetime"
        RS.Open "ALTER TABLE " & CurrentTable & " ADD " & FieldName &
                      " Datetime", CN

    Case "bit"
        RS.Open "ALTER TABLE " & CurrentTable & " ADD " & FieldName &
                      " Bit", CN

    Case Else
        MsgBox "Unrecognized Data Type, please try this operation again."
        Exit Sub

End Select

TableID = CurrentIndex
```

```
Dim RSFields As ADOCE.Recordset
Set RSFields = CreateObject("ADOCE.Recordset.3.0")
'View all Fields looking for the indexed fields

'View all Indexes
RS.Open "MSysIndexes", CN
While Not RS.EOF

    'Only look at Indexes in the current table
    If (TableID = CLng(RS("TableID"))) Then

        IndexName = RS("IndexName")
        FieldID = RS("FieldID")

        RSFields.Open "MSysFields", CN
        While Not RSFields.EOF

            If RSFields("FieldID") = FieldID And RSFields("TableID") =
            TableID Then
                IndexedFieldName = RSFields("FieldName")

            End If
            RSFields.MoveNext
        Wend
        RSFields.Close

    End If

    RS.MoveNext
Wend
RS.Close
Set RSFields = Nothing

'A keyset-based, forward and backward, read and write Recordset
RS.Open CurrentTable, CN

'Remove existing data from Grid
GridCtrl1.Redraw = False
For i = 1 To GridCtrl1.Rows
    GridCtrl1.RemoveItem 0
Next
```

```
GridCtrl1.Cols = 5
GridCtrl1.ColWidth(0) = 110 * Len("Field Name")
GridCtrl1.ColWidth(1) = 110 * Len("Data Type")
GridCtrl1.ColWidth(2) = 110 * Len("Length")
GridCtrl1.ColWidth(3) = 110 * Len("Indexed")
GridCtrl1.ColWidth(4) = 110 * Len("Index Name")


GridCtrl1.AddItem "Field Name" & vbTab & "Data Type" & vbTab & "Length" &
                          vbTab & "Indexed" & vbTab & "Index Name"


'View Fields
For i = 0 To RS.Fields.Count - 1

    'Convert the Field Type number
    'into a meaningful string
    Select Case RS.Fields(i).Type
        Case 202
            FieldType = "Varchar"
        Case 203
            FieldType = "Text"
        Case 204
            FieldType = "Varbinary"
        Case 205
            FieldType = "Long Varbinary"
        Case 3
            FieldType = "Integer"
        Case 2
            FieldType = "Smallint"
        Case 5
            FieldType = "Float"
        Case 7
            FieldType = "Datetime"
        Case 11
            FieldType = "Bit"
    End Select

    'Get the Field Name
    FieldName = RS.Fields(i).Name

    'Get the Field Length
    FieldLength = RS.Fields(i).DefinedSize
```

```
            If FieldName = IndexedFieldName Then
                GridCtrl1.AddItem FieldName & vbTab & FieldType & vbTab &
                                FieldLength & vbTab & "Yes" & vbTab & IndexName
            Else
                GridCtrl1.AddItem FieldName & vbTab & FieldType & vbTab &
                                        FieldLength & vbTab & "No" & vbTab & ""
            End If

        Next
        RS.Close

        GridCtrl1.Redraw = True

        Set RS = Nothing

    Else
        MsgBox "You must enter a Field Name and a Data Type."
        Exit Sub
    End If


End Sub
```

Renaming a Field

A field is renamed when the user clicks the desired field in the Grid and then selects the Rename Selected Field menu item. Things start off with the obligatory check to make sure the user has selected a cell in the Grid other than the column headers. The field name is captured and then the user is prompted to enter a new field name using an InputBox. The field is then renamed with the use of the ALTER TABLE statement along with the RENAME and TO parameters. The rest of the code is the same as that in the ViewMetaData Sub. Create a Sub called "RenameSelectedField()" and add the following code:

```
Private Sub RenameSelectedField()

    On Error Resume Next

    Dim FieldName As String
    Dim NewFieldName As String
    Dim DataType As String
    Dim DataLength As Integer
```

```
Dim i As Integer
Dim FieldType As String
Dim IndexName As String
Dim FieldID As Integer
Dim TableID As Long
Dim IndexedFieldName As String
Dim Indexed As String
Dim FieldLength As Integer

'Ensure that the following code is executed
'only if the user clicks on a valid nonheader row.
If GridCtrl1.RowSel > 0 Then

    'Get the name of the field to rename
    FieldName = GridCtrl1.TextMatrix(GridCtrl1.RowSel, 0)

    'Get the new name
    NewFieldName = InputBox("Enter a new Field Name.", "Rename Field")

    If NewFieldName <> "" Then

        'Create Recordset Object
        Dim RS As ADOCE.Recordset
        Set RS = CreateObject("ADOCE.Recordset.3.0")

        RS.Open "ALTER TABLE " & CurrentTable & " RENAME " & FieldName &
                    " TO " & NewFieldName, CN

        TableID = CurrentIndex

        Dim RSFields As ADOCE.Recordset
        Set RSFields = CreateObject("ADOCE.Recordset.3.0")

        'View all Indexes
        RS.Open "MSysIndexes", CN
        While Not RS.EOF

            'Only look at Indexes in the current table
            If (TableID = CLng(RS("TableID"))) Then

                IndexName = RS("IndexName")
                FieldID = RS("FieldID")
```

```
                        RSFields.Open "MSysFields", CN
                        While Not RSFields.EOF

                            If RSFields("FieldID") = FieldID And RSFields("TableID") =
                            TableID Then
                                IndexedFieldName = RSFields("FieldName")

                            End If
                            RSFields.MoveNext
                        Wend
                        RSFields.Close

                End If

            RS.MoveNext
        Wend
        RS.Close

        Set RSFields = Nothing

        'A keyset-based, forward and backward, read and write Recordset
        RS.Open CurrentTable, CN

        'Remove existing data from Grid
        GridCtrl1.Redraw = False
        For i = 1 To GridCtrl1.Rows
            GridCtrl1.RemoveItem 0
        Next

        GridCtrl1.Cols = 5
        GridCtrl1.ColWidth(0) = 110 * Len("Field Name")
        GridCtrl1.ColWidth(1) = 110 * Len("Data Type")
        GridCtrl1.ColWidth(2) = 110 * Len("Length")
        GridCtrl1.ColWidth(3) = 110 * Len("Indexed")
        GridCtrl1.ColWidth(4) = 110 * Len("Index Name")

        GridCtrl1.AddItem "Field Name" & vbTab & "Data Type" & vbTab &
        "Length" & vbTab & "Indexed" & vbTab & "Index Name"

        'View Fields
        For i = 0 To RS.Fields.Count - 1

            'Convert the Field Type number
```

```
        'into a meaningful string
        Select Case RS.Fields(i).Type
            Case 202
                FieldType = "Varchar"
            Case 203
                FieldType = "Text"
            Case 204
                FieldType = "Varbinary"
            Case 205
                FieldType = "Long Varbinary"
            Case 3
                FieldType = "Integer"
            Case 2
                FieldType = "Smallint"
            Case 5
                FieldType = "Float"
            Case 7
                FieldType = "Datetime"
            Case 11
                FieldType = "Bit"
        End Select

        'Get the Field Name
        FieldName = RS.Fields(i).Name

        'Get the Field Length
        FieldLength = RS.Fields(i).DefinedSize

        If FieldName = IndexedFieldName Then
            GridCtrl1.AddItem FieldName & vbTab & FieldType & vbTab &
            FieldLength & vbTab & "Yes" & vbTab & IndexName
        Else
            GridCtrl1.AddItem FieldName & vbTab & FieldType & vbTab &
            FieldLength & vbTab & "No" & vbTab & ""
        End If

    Next
    RS.Close

GridCtrl1.Redraw = True

Set RS = Nothing
Else
    MsgBox "You must enter a new Field Name."
```

```
            Exit Sub
End If

            End If


End Sub
```

Moving a Field Up

There will come a time in your life when you realize you've built a table and you don't like the order in which the fields appear. Luckily, all is not lost. You can move a field up in the order by clicking it in the Grid and then selecting the Move Selected Field Up menu item. The field name you want to move as well as the field name that resides above it is captured for use. You then use the Recordset to execute the ALTER TABLE statement along with the MOVE and BEFORE parameters to get the job done. Once the field has been moved, the same code that's used in the ViewMetaData Sub is executed to refresh the Grid and reveal the field's new station in life. Create a Sub called "MoveSelectedFieldUp()" and add the following code:

```
Private Sub MoveSelectedFieldUp()

    On Error Resume Next

    Dim FieldName As String
    Dim FieldAbove As String
    Dim DataType As String
    Dim DataLength As Integer
    Dim i As Integer
    Dim FieldType As String
    Dim IndexName As String
    Dim FieldID As Integer
    Dim TableID As Long
    Dim IndexedFieldName As String
    Dim Indexed As String
    Dim FieldLength As Integer

    'Ensure that the following code is executed
    'only if the user clicks a valid nonheader row.
    If GridCtrl1.RowSel > 1 Then

        'Get the name of the field to move up
```

```
FieldName = GridCtrl1.TextMatrix(GridCtrl1.RowSel, 0)

'Get the name of the field above the selected field
FieldAbove = GridCtrl1.TextMatrix(GridCtrl1.RowSel - 1, 0)


If FieldAbove <> "" Then

    'Create Recordset Object
    Dim RS As ADOCE.Recordset
    Set RS = CreateObject("ADOCE.Recordset.3.0")

    RS.Open "ALTER TABLE " & CurrentTable & " MOVE " & FieldName & _
                " BEFORE " & FieldAbove, CN


    TableID = CurrentIndex

    Dim RSFields As ADOCE.Recordset
    Set RSFields = CreateObject("ADOCE.Recordset.3.0")

    'View all Indexes
    RS.Open "MSysIndexes", CN
    While Not RS.EOF

        'Only look at Indexes in the current table
        If (TableID = CLng(RS("TableID"))) Then

            IndexName = RS("IndexName")
            FieldID = RS("FieldID")

            RSFields.Open "MSysFields", CN
            While Not RSFields.EOF

                If RSFields("FieldID") = FieldID And RSFields("TableID") = _
                TableID Then
                    IndexedFieldName = RSFields("FieldName")

                End If
                RSFields.MoveNext
            Wend
            RSFields.Close

        End If
```

```
            RS.MoveNext
Wend
RS.Close

Set RSFields = Nothing

RS.Open CurrentTable, CN

'Remove existing data from Grid
GridCtrl1.Redraw = False
For i = 1 To GridCtrl1.Rows
    GridCtrl1.RemoveItem 0
Next

GridCtrl1.Cols = 5
GridCtrl1.ColWidth(0) = 110 * Len("Field Name")
GridCtrl1.ColWidth(1) = 110 * Len("Data Type")
GridCtrl1.ColWidth(2) = 110 * Len("Length")
GridCtrl1.ColWidth(3) = 110 * Len("Indexed")
GridCtrl1.ColWidth(4) = 110 * Len("Index Name")

GridCtrl1.AddItem "Field Name" & vbTab & "Data Type" & vbTab &
  "Length" & vbTab & "Indexed" & vbTab & "Index Name"

'View all Fields in Table
For i = 0 To RS.Fields.Count - 1

    'Convert the Field Type number
    'into a meaningful string
    Select Case RS.Fields(i).Type
        Case 202
            FieldType = "Varchar"
        Case 203
            FieldType = "Text"
        Case 204
            FieldType = "Varbinary"
        Case 205
            FieldType = "Long Varbinary"
        Case 3
            FieldType = "Integer"
        Case 2
            FieldType = "Smallint"
        Case 5
            FieldType = "Float"
```

```
            Case 7
                FieldType = "Datetime"
            Case 11
                FieldType = "Bit"
        End Select

        'Get the Field Name
        FieldName = RS.Fields(i).Name

        'Get the Field Length
        FieldLength = RS.Fields(i).DefinedSize

        If FieldName = IndexedFieldName Then
            GridCtrl1.AddItem FieldName & vbTab & FieldType & vbTab &
                FieldLength & vbTab & "Yes" & vbTab & IndexName
        Else
            GridCtrl1.AddItem FieldName & vbTab & FieldType & vbTab &
                FieldLength & vbTab & "No" & vbTab & ""
        End If

    Next
    RS.Close

    GridCtrl1.Redraw = True

    Set RS = Nothing
    Else
        MsgBox "You can't move your field above the first position."
        Exit Sub
    End If

    End If

End Sub
```

Moving a Field Down

One good turn deserves another, so you can also move a field down in the field order by selecting the field to move in the Grid and then choosing the Move Selected Field Down menu item. This code works exactly like the code to move a field up, except that this time you capture the name of the field that's two rows below the selected field.

By now you're probably wondering why I didn't combine this code with the code to move a field up. Well, as I said at the beginning of this chapter, I'm providing a foundation and I'm looking to you to improve upon it. That said, create a Sub called "MoveSelectedFieldDown()" and add the following code:

```
Private Sub MoveSelectedFieldDown()

    On Error Resume Next

    Dim FieldName As String
    Dim FieldBelow As String
    Dim DataType As String
    Dim DataLength As Integer
    Dim i As Integer
    Dim FieldType As String
    Dim IndexName As String
    Dim FieldID As Integer
    Dim TableID As Long
    Dim IndexedFieldName As String
    Dim Indexed As String
    Dim FieldLength As Integer

    'Ensure that the following code is executed
    'only if the user clicks a valid nonheader row.
    If GridCtrl1.RowSel > 0 Then

        'Get the name of the field to move down
        FieldName = GridCtrl1.TextMatrix(GridCtrl1.RowSel, 0)

        'Get the name of the field below the selected field
        FieldBelow = GridCtrl1.TextMatrix(GridCtrl1.RowSel + 2, 0)

        If FieldBelow <> "" Then

            'Create Recordset Object
            Dim RS As ADOCE.Recordset
            Set RS = CreateObject("ADOCE.Recordset.3.0")

            RS.Open "ALTER TABLE " & CurrentTable & " MOVE " & FieldName & _
                        " BEFORE " & FieldBelow, CN

            TableID = CurrentIndex

            Dim RSFields As ADOCE.Recordset
```

```
Set RSFields = CreateObject("ADOCE.Recordset.3.0")


'View all Indexes
RS.Open "MSysIndexes", CN
While Not RS.EOF

    'Only look at Indexes in the current table
    If (TableID = CLng(RS("TableID"))) Then

        IndexName = RS("IndexName")
        FieldID = RS("FieldID")

        RSFields.Open "MSysFields", CN
        While Not RSFields.EOF

            If RSFields("FieldID") = FieldID And RSFields("TableID") =
            TableID Then
                IndexedFieldName = RSFields("FieldName")

            End If
            RSFields.MoveNext
        Wend
        RSFields.Close

    End If

    RS.MoveNext
Wend
RS.Close

Set RSFields = Nothing

RS.Open CurrentTable, CN

'Remove existing data from Grid
GridCtrl1.Redraw = False
For i = 1 To GridCtrl1.Rows
    GridCtrl1.RemoveItem 0
Next

GridCtrl1.Cols = 5
GridCtrl1.ColWidth(0) = 110 * Len("Field Name")
GridCtrl1.ColWidth(1) = 110 * Len("Data Type")
```

```
GridCtrl1.ColWidth(2) = 110 * Len("Length")
GridCtrl1.ColWidth(3) = 110 * Len("Indexed")
GridCtrl1.ColWidth(4) = 110 * Len("Index Name")

GridCtrl1.AddItem "Field Name" & vbTab & "Data Type" & vbTab &
"Length" & vbTab & "Indexed" & vbTab & "Index Name"

'View all Fields in Table
For i = 0 To RS.Fields.Count - 1

    'Convert the Field Type number
    'into a meaningful string
    Select Case RS.Fields(i).Type
        Case 202
            FieldType = "Varchar"
        Case 203
            FieldType = "Text"
        Case 204
            FieldType = "Varbinary"
        Case 205
            FieldType = "Long Varbinary"
        Case 3
            FieldType = "Integer"
        Case 2
            FieldType = "Smallint"
        Case 5
            FieldType = "Float"
        Case 7
            FieldType = "Datetime"
        Case 11
            FieldType = "Bit"
    End Select

    'Get the Field Name
    FieldName = RS.Fields(i).Name

    'Get the Field Length
     FieldLength = RS.Fields(i).DefinedSize


    If FieldName = IndexedFieldName Then
        GridCtrl1.AddItem FieldName & vbTab & FieldType & vbTab &
         FieldLength & vbTab & "Yes" & vbTab & IndexName
    Else
```

```
            GridCtrl1.AddItem FieldName & vbTab & FieldType & vbTab &
            FieldLength & vbTab & "No" & vbTab & ""
        End If


    Next
    RS.Close

    GridCtrl1.Redraw = True

    Set RS = Nothing
Else
    MsgBox "You can't move your field below the last position."
    Exit Sub
End If


End If


End Sub
```

Deleting a Field

Clicking the field to delete in the Grid and selecting the Delete Selected Field menu item deletes a field. This is a simple one. With the field name in hand, the ALTER TABLE statement is called with the DROP parameter. After that, code similar to that found in the ViewMetaData Sub code is executed to refresh the Grid where the deleted field will be noticeably absent. Create a Sub called "DeleteSelectedField()" and add the following code:

```
Private Sub DeleteSelectedField()

    On Error Resume Next

    Dim FieldName As String
    Dim DataType As String
    Dim DataLength As Integer
    Dim i As Integer
    Dim FieldType As String
    Dim IndexName As String
    Dim FieldID As Integer
    Dim TableID As Long
    Dim IndexedFieldName As String
    Dim Indexed As String
```

```
Dim FieldLength As Integer

'Ensure that the following code is executed
'only if the user clicks a valid nonheader row.
If GridCtrl1.RowSel > 0 Then

    'Get the name of the field to delete
    FieldName = GridCtrl1.TextMatrix(GridCtrl1.RowSel, 0)

    'Create Recordset Object
    Dim RS As ADOCE.Recordset
    Set RS = CreateObject("ADOCE.Recordset.3.0")

    RS.Open "ALTER TABLE " & CurrentTable & " DROP " & FieldName, CN

    TableID = CurrentIndex

    Dim RSFields As ADOCE.Recordset
    Set RSFields = CreateObject("ADOCE.Recordset.3.0")

    'View all Indexes
    RS.Open "MSysIndexes", CN
    While Not RS.EOF

        'Only look at Indexes in the current table
        If (TableID = CLng(RS("TableID"))) Then

            IndexName = RS("IndexName")
            FieldID = RS("FieldID")

            RSFields.Open "MSysFields", CN
            While Not RSFields.EOF

                If RSFields("FieldID") = FieldID And RSFields("TableID") =
                TableID Then
                    IndexedFieldName = RSFields("FieldName")

                End If
                RSFields.MoveNext
            Wend
            RSFields.Close

        End If
```

```
        RS.MoveNext
Wend
RS.Close
Set RSFields = Nothing

'A keyset-based, forward and backward, read and write Recordset
RS.Open CurrentTable, CN

'Remove existing data from Grid
GridCtrl1.Redraw = False
For i = 1 To GridCtrl1.Rows
    GridCtrl1.RemoveItem 0
Next

GridCtrl1.Cols = 5
GridCtrl1.ColWidth(0) = 110 * Len("Field Name")
GridCtrl1.ColWidth(1) = 110 * Len("Data Type")
GridCtrl1.ColWidth(2) = 110 * Len("Length")
GridCtrl1.ColWidth(3) = 110 * Len("Indexed")
GridCtrl1.ColWidth(4) = 110 * Len("Index Name")

GridCtrl1.AddItem "Field Name" & vbTab & "Data Type" & vbTab & "Length" &
 vbTab & "Indexed" & vbTab & "Index Name"

'View all Fields in Table
For i = 0 To RS.Fields.Count - 1

    'Convert the Field Type number
    'into a meaningful string
    Select Case RS.Fields(i).Type
        Case 202
            FieldType = "Varchar"
        Case 203
            FieldType = "Text"
        Case 204
            FieldType = "Varbinary"
        Case 205
            FieldType = "Long Varbinary"
        Case 3
            FieldType = "Integer"
        Case 2
            FieldType = "Smallint"
        Case 5
            FieldType = "Float"
```

```
                    Case 7
                        FieldType = "Datetime"
                    Case 11
                        FieldType = "Bit"
            End Select

            'Get the Field Name
            FieldName = RS.Fields(i).Name

            'Get the Field Length
            FieldLength = RS.Fields(i).DefinedSize

            If FieldName = IndexedFieldName Then
                GridCtrl1.AddItem FieldName & vbTab & FieldType & vbTab &
                    FieldLength & vbTab & "Yes" & vbTab & IndexName
            Else
                GridCtrl1.AddItem FieldName & vbTab & FieldType & vbTab &
                    FieldLength & vbTab & "No" & vbTab & ""
            End If

        Next
        RS.Close

        GridCtrl1.Redraw = True

        Set RS = Nothing

    End If

End Sub
```

Working with Indexes

You can add or delete an index from a Pocket Access table with ADOCE. This functionality is made available on the Fields menu because it's a feature of the Grid's Metadata view.

Adding an Index

You can add an index to a table by clicking the field to index in the Grid and then selecting the Add Index menu item. First, the field name to index is captured

from the Grid and then the user is prompted to enter a name for the new index in
an InputBox. Next, the CREATE INDEX statement is executed using the field
name, index name, and table name. After that, the metadata Grid is refreshed
with code similar to that found in the ViewMetaData Sub. Create a Sub called
"AddSelectedIndex()" and add the following code:

```
Private Sub AddSelectedIndex()

    On Error Resume Next

    Dim FieldName As String
    Dim NewIndexName As String
    Dim DataType As String
    Dim DataLength As Integer
    Dim i As Integer
    Dim FieldType As String
    Dim IndexName As String
    Dim FieldID As Integer
    Dim TableID As Long
    Dim IndexedFieldName As String
    Dim Indexed As String
    Dim FieldLength As Integer

    'Ensure that the following code is executed
    'only if the user clicks a valid nonheader row.
    If GridCtrl1.RowSel > 0 Then

        'Get the name of the field to delete
        FieldName = GridCtrl1.TextMatrix(GridCtrl1.RowSel, 0)

        NewIndexName = InputBox("Enter a new Index Name.", "Add Index")

        If NewIndexName <> "" Then

            'Create Recordset Object
            Dim RS As ADOCE.Recordset
            Set RS = CreateObject("ADOCE.Recordset.3.0")

            RS.Open "CREATE INDEX " & NewIndexName & " ON " & CurrentTable &
                        "(" & FieldName & ")", CN

            TableID = CurrentIndex

            Dim RSFields As ADOCE.Recordset
```

```
            Set RSFields = CreateObject("ADOCE.Recordset.3.0")

            'View all Indexes
            RS.Open "MSysIndexes", CN
            While Not RS.EOF

                'Only look at Indexes in the current table
                If (TableID = CLng(RS("TableID"))) Then

                    IndexName = RS("IndexName")
                    FieldID = RS("FieldID")

                    RSFields.Open "MSysFields", CN
                    While Not RSFields.EOF

                        If RSFields("FieldID") = FieldID And RSFields("TableID") =
                        TableID Then
                            IndexedFieldName = RSFields("FieldName")

                        End If
                        RSFields.MoveNext
                    Wend
                    RSFields.Close

                End If

                RS.MoveNext
            Wend
            RS.Close
            Set RSFields = Nothing

            RS.Open CurrentTable, CN

            'Remove existing data from Grid
            GridCtrl1.Redraw = False
            For i = 1 To GridCtrl1.Rows
                GridCtrl1.RemoveItem 0
            Next

            GridCtrl1.Cols = 5
            GridCtrl1.ColWidth(0) = 110 * Len("Field Name")
            GridCtrl1.ColWidth(1) = 110 * Len("Data Type")
            GridCtrl1.ColWidth(2) = 110 * Len("Length")
```

```
GridCtrl1.ColWidth(3) = 110 * Len("Indexed")
GridCtrl1.ColWidth(4) = 110 * Len("Index Name")

GridCtrl1.AddItem "Field Name" & vbTab & "Data Type" & vbTab &
"Length" & vbTab & "Indexed" & vbTab & "Index Name"

'View all Fields in Table
For i = 0 To RS.Fields.Count - 1

    'Convert the Field Type number
    'into a meaningful string
    Select Case RS.Fields(i).Type
        Case 202
            FieldType = "Varchar"
        Case 203
            FieldType = "Text"
        Case 204
            FieldType = "Varbinary"
        Case 205
            FieldType = "Long Varbinary"
        Case 3
            FieldType = "Integer"
        Case 2
            FieldType = "Smallint"
        Case 5
            FieldType = "Float"
        Case 7
            FieldType = "Datetime"
        Case 11
            FieldType = "Bit"
    End Select

    'Get the Field Name
    FieldName = RS.Fields(i).Name

    'Get the Field Length
    FieldLength = RS.Fields(i).DefinedSize

    If FieldName = IndexedFieldName Then
        GridCtrl1.AddItem FieldName & vbTab & FieldType & vbTab &
         FieldLength & vbTab & "Yes" & vbTab & IndexName
    Else
        GridCtrl1.AddItem FieldName & vbTab & FieldType & vbTab &
        FieldLength & vbTab & "No" & vbTab & ""
```

```
                    End If


            Next
            RS.Close


            GridCtrl1.Redraw = True


            Set RS = Nothing
        Else
            MsgBox "You must enter a new Index Name."
            Exit Sub
        End If


    End If


End Sub
```

Deleting an Index

You can delete an index by clicking the indexed field in the Grid and then selecting the Delete Selected Index menu item. With the row of the field containing the index selected, you look across to the fifth column to retrieve the index name. After that, it's a simple matter of executing the DROP INDEX statement along with the table and index name. The rest of the code is similar to the code found in the ViewMetaData Sub. When the Grid is refreshed, there will be a blank cell in the Grid where the index name once resided. Create a Sub called "DeleteSelectedIndex()" and add the following code:

```
Private Sub DeleteSelectedIndex()

    On Error Resume Next

    Dim FieldName As String
    Dim SelectedIndexName As String
    Dim DataType As String
    Dim DataLength As Integer
    Dim i As Integer
    Dim FieldType As String
    Dim IndexName As String
    Dim FieldID As Integer
    Dim TableID As Long
    Dim IndexedFieldName As String
```

```
Dim Indexed As String
Dim FieldLength As Integer

'Ensure that the following code is executed
'only if the user clicks a valid nonheader row.
If GridCtrl1.RowSel > 0 Then

    SelectedIndexName = GridCtrl1.TextMatrix(GridCtrl1.RowSel, 4)

    'Create Recordset Object
    Dim RS As ADOCE.Recordset
    Set RS = CreateObject("ADOCE.Recordset.3.0")

    RS.Open "DROP INDEX " & CurrentTable & "." & SelectedIndexName, CN

    TableID = CurrentIndex

    Dim RSFields As ADOCE.Recordset
    Set RSFields = CreateObject("ADOCE.Recordset.3.0")

    'View all Indexes
    RS.Open "MSysIndexes", CN
    While Not RS.EOF

        'Only look at Indexes in the current table
        If (TableID = CLng(RS("TableID"))) Then

            IndexName = RS("IndexName")
            FieldID = RS("FieldID")

            RSFields.Open "MSysFields", CN
            While Not RSFields.EOF

                If RSFields("FieldID") = FieldID And RSFields("TableID") =
                TableID Then
                    IndexedFieldName = RSFields("FieldName")

                End If
                RSFields.MoveNext
            Wend
            RSFields.Close

        End If
```

```
        RS.MoveNext
Wend
RS.Close

Set RSFields = Nothing

'A keyset-based, forward and backward, read and write Recordset
RS.Open CurrentTable, CN

'Remove existing data from Grid
GridCtrl1.Redraw = False
For i = 1 To GridCtrl1.Rows
    GridCtrl1.RemoveItem 0
Next

GridCtrl1.Cols = 5
GridCtrl1.ColWidth(0) = 110 * Len("Field Name")
GridCtrl1.ColWidth(1) = 110 * Len("Data Type")
GridCtrl1.ColWidth(2) = 110 * Len("Length")
GridCtrl1.ColWidth(3) = 110 * Len("Indexed")
GridCtrl1.ColWidth(4) = 110 * Len("Index Name")

GridCtrl1.AddItem "Field Name" & vbTab & "Data Type" & vbTab & "Length" &
 vbTab & "Indexed" & vbTab & "Index Name"

'View all Fields in Table
For i = 0 To RS.Fields.Count - 1

    'Convert the Field Type number
    'into a meaningful string
    Select Case RS.Fields(i).Type
        Case 202
            FieldType = "Varchar"
        Case 203
            FieldType = "Text"
        Case 204
            FieldType = "Varbinary"
        Case 205
            FieldType = "Long Varbinary"
        Case 3
            FieldType = "Integer"
        Case 2
            FieldType = "Smallint"
```

```
            Case 5
                FieldType = "Float"
            Case 7
                FieldType = "Datetime"
            Case 11
                FieldType = "Bit"
        End Select

        'Get the Field Name
        FieldName = RS.Fields(i).Name

        'Get the Field Length
        FieldLength = RS.Fields(i).DefinedSize

        If FieldName = IndexedFieldName Then
            GridCtrl1.AddItem FieldName & vbTab & FieldType & vbTab &
            FieldLength & vbTab & "Yes" & vbTab & IndexName
        Else
            GridCtrl1.AddItem FieldName & vbTab & FieldType & vbTab &
            FieldLength & vbTab & "No" & vbTab & ""
        End If

    Next
    RS.Close

    GridCtrl1.Redraw = True

    Set RS = Nothing

    End If

End Sub
```

Working with Data

Up until now, you've focused on the DDL or construction part of working with
Pocket Access databases. It's interesting to note that with as much time and effort
you've put into building that side of things, the manipulation of tables, fields, and
indexes constitute the smallest amount of time spent with any given database.
What you really want to do is view, add, update, delete, query, and sort data.
You'll be able to do that with some help from the versatile Grid control and the
Data menu, as shown in Figure 7-6.

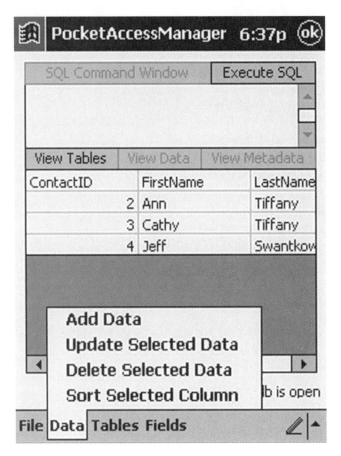

Figure 7-6. The Data menu

Viewing Data

A user can view the data for any given table by clicking that table in the Grid and then clicking the View Data button. The first thing that happens is that the table name is captured and used to open a Recordset of data containing all that table's data. Next, the Grid is emptied and then rebuilt with metadata and data retrieved by iterating through the Fields Collection of the table's Recordset. Now you have a complete view of any given table's data. Create a Sub called "ViewData()" and add the following code:

```
Private Sub ViewData()

    On Error Resume Next

    'Declare variables
    Dim i As Integer
```

```
Dim ColumnNames As String
Dim ColumnValues As String

'Ensure that the following code is executed
'only if the user clicks a valid nonheader row.
If GridCtrl1.RowSel > 0 Then

    'Create Recordset Object
    Dim RS As ADOCE.Recordset
    Set RS = CreateObject("ADOCE.Recordset.3.0")

    'Return the data found in the cell at the intersection
    'of the selected row and column 0
    RS.Open GridCtrl1.TextMatrix(GridCtrl1.RowSel, 0), CN, adOpenKeyset,
                                adLockOptimistic, adCmdTable

    'This allows Add, Update, and Delete to know the table name being viewed
    CurrentTable = GridCtrl1.TextMatrix(GridCtrl1.RowSel, 0)
    CurrentIndex = CLng(GridCtrl1.TextMatrix(GridCtrl1.RowSel, 1))

    'Remove existing data from Grid
    GridCtrl1.Redraw = False
    For i = 1 To GridCtrl1.Rows
        GridCtrl1.RemoveItem 0
    Next

    'Set the Grid columns equal to the field count
    GridCtrl1.Cols = RS.Fields.Count

    'Get the column names
    For i = 0 To RS.Fields.Count - 1
        GridCtrl1.ColWidth(i) = 1300 '110 * Len(RS.Fields(i).Name)
        ColumnNames = ColumnNames & RS.Fields(i).Name & vbTab
    Next

    'Add the column headers to the Grid
    GridCtrl1.AddItem ColumnNames

    'Loop through the Recordset
    While Not RS.EOF

        'Get the column values for this row
        For i = 0 To RS.Fields.Count - 1
```

```
                ColumnValues = ColumnValues & RS.Fields(i).Value & vbTab
            Next

            'Add the column values to the row
            GridCtrl1.AddItem ColumnValues

            'Set ColumnValues to a zero-length string
            'so it can be refilled with the next row
            ColumnValues = ""

            RS.MoveNext
        Wend

        GridCtrl1.Redraw = True

        'Close the Recordset
        RS.Close

        cmdDataView.Enabled = False
        cmdMetaDataView.Enabled = False
        cmdExecuteSQL.Enabled = True

        DataMenu.Items(1).Enabled = True       'Add Data
        DataMenu.Items(2).Enabled = True       'Update Selected Data
        DataMenu.Items(3).Enabled = True       'Delete Selected Data
        DataMenu.Items(4).Enabled = True       'Sort Selected Column

        TableMenu.Items(1).Enabled = False      'Add Table
        TableMenu.Items(2).Enabled = False      'Delete Selected Table
        TableMenu.Items(3).Enabled = False      'Rename Selected Table

        FieldMenu.Items(1).Enabled = False      'Add Field
        FieldMenu.Items(2).Enabled = False      'Delete Selected Field
        FieldMenu.Items(3).Enabled = False      'Rename Field
        FieldMenu.Items(4).Enabled = False      'Move Selected Field Up
        FieldMenu.Items(5).Enabled = False      'Move Selected Field Down
        FieldMenu.Items(7).Enabled = False      'Add Index
        FieldMenu.Items(8).Enabled = False      'Delete Selected Index

        Set RS = Nothing

    End If

End Sub
```

Adding Data

If a user wants to add a row of data to the table he or she is currently viewing, all that user needs to do is select the Add Data menu item. Adding data to a dynamically generated Grid of data is one of the most complicated operations performed in this application. If you remember, you used code similar to this back in Chapter 6, so it shouldn't be completely foreign to you. One of the problems you faced was dealing with autoincrementing fields because Pocket Access doesn't support them. During the process of adding data, whenever you encountered an Integer field, you ended up asking the user if that field was autoincrementing. I promised that you would be a little more scientific the second time around, so now you use the familiar index determination code found in all the field/metadata Subs to retrieve the field with an index. In your new and improved code, a field must be both indexed and an Integer in order to ask the user if the field is autoincrementing. You start out with an AddNew method and from there you just prompt the user with InputBoxes to enter data for the given field. Finally, you update the table with the new data, requery the database, and then refill the Grid where the new row of data will be visible. Create a Sub called "AddData()" and add the following code:

```
Private Sub AddData()

    On Error Resume Next

    'Declare variables
    Dim i As Integer
    Dim ColumnNames As String
    Dim ColumnValues As String
    Dim IndexName As String
    Dim FieldID As Integer
    Dim IndexedFieldName As String

    'Create 2 Recordset Objects
    Dim RS As ADOCE.Recordset
    Dim RSFields As ADOCE.Recordset
    Set RS = CreateObject("ADOCE.Recordset.3.0")
    Set RSFields = CreateObject("ADOCE.Recordset.3.0")

    'View all Indexes
    RS.Open "MSysIndexes", CN
    While Not RS.EOF

        'Only look at Indexes in the current table
```

```
        If (CurrentIndex = CLng(RS("TableID"))) Then
            'Get index name and field id
            IndexName = RS("IndexName")
            FieldID = RS("FieldID")

            'View all fields
            RSFields.Open "MSysFields", CN
            While Not RSFields.EOF
                If RSFields("FieldID") = FieldID And RSFields("TableID") =
                CurrentIndex Then
                    'Get name of indexed column
                    IndexedFieldName = RSFields("FieldName")
                End If
                RSFields.MoveNext
            Wend
            RSFields.Close

    End If
    RS.MoveNext
Wend
RS.Close
Set RSFields = Nothing

'Open the selected table
RS.Open CurrentTable, CN, adOpenKeyset, adLockOptimistic, adCmdTable

'Call the AddNew method
RS.AddNew

'Get dynamic user input
For i = 0 To RS.Fields.Count - 1

    'If the field is indexed and an integer then ask if column is
autoincrementing. . .
    If RS.Fields(i).Name = IndexedFieldName And RS.Fields(i).Type =
    adInteger Then

        'Ask the user if the field is autoincrementing
        If MsgBox("Is " & RS.Fields(i).Name & " an autoincrementing field?",
        vbYesNoCancel) = vbYes Then

            'Code to Auto Increment
            Dim AutoNumber As Integer
            Dim Identity As ADOCE.Recordset
```

```
                Set Identity = CreateObject("ADOCE.Recordset.3.0")
                Identity.Open "SELECT " & RS.Fields(i).Name & " FROM " &
                CurrentTable & " ORDER BY " & RS.Fields(i).Name & " DESC", CN
                If Not RS.BOF And Not RS.EOF Then
                    AutoNumber = CInt(Identity(0)) + 1
                Else
                    AutoNumber = 1
                End If
                Identity.Close
                Set Identity = Nothing

                'Set new field equal to a new autoincremented number
                RS(RS.Fields(i).Name) = AutoNumber

            Else

                'Set new field equal to user input
                RS(RS.Fields(i).Name) = InputBox(RS.Fields(i).Name, "Add")

            End If

        Else

            'Set new field equal to user input
            RS(RS.Fields(i).Name) = InputBox(RS.Fields(i).Name, "Add")

        End If

Next

'Ask user if they want the record added
If MsgBox("Do you wish to add this record?", vbYesNoCancel) = vbYes Then
    RS.Update
Else
    RS.CancelUpdate
    MsgBox "No new record added."
End If

'Query the database again to refresh the Grid
RS.Requery

'Remove existing data from Grid
GridCtrl1.Redraw = False
For i = 1 To GridCtrl1.Rows
```

```
            GridCtrl1.RemoveItem 0
    Next

    'Set the Grid columns equal to the field count
    GridCtrl1.Cols = RS.Fields.Count

    'Get the column names
    For i = 0 To RS.Fields.Count - 1
        ColumnNames = ColumnNames & RS.Fields(i).Name & vbTab
    Next

    GridCtrl1.Redraw = False

    'Add the column headers to the Grid
    GridCtrl1.AddItem ColumnNames

    'Loop through the Recordset
    While Not RS.EOF

        'Get the column values for this row
        For i = 0 To RS.Fields.Count - 1
            ColumnValues = ColumnValues & RS.Fields(i).Value & vbTab
        Next

        'Add the column values to the row
        GridCtrl1.AddItem ColumnValues

        'Set ColumnValues to a zero-length string
        'so it can be refilled with the next row
        ColumnValues = ""

        RS.MoveNext

    Wend

    GridCtrl1.Redraw = True

    RS.Close
    Set RS = Nothing

End Sub
```

Updating Data

Whenever you find yourself with a cell of data in the Grid that needs changing, just click that cell and select the Update Selected Data menu item. The first thing you do in the code is build a query that returns just the column and row that corresponds to the cell clicked in the Grid. With a Recordset containing only one item, you prompt the user to enter a new value for this item using an InputBox. If everything looks fine to the user, the Update method is called to actually change the value in the table. The Grid is then refreshed using the same kind of code found in the ViewData Sub. Create a Sub called "UpdateSelectedData()" and add the following code:

```
Private Sub UpdateSelectedData()

    On Error Resume Next

    'Declare variables
    Dim i As Integer
    Dim ColumnNames As String
    Dim ColumnValues As String
    Dim SQL As String

    If GridCtrl1.RowSel > 0 Then

        If GridCtrl1.TextMatrix(GridCtrl1.RowSel, GridCtrl1.ColSel) <> "" Then

            'Build a query to return just the column and value
            'reflected in the user's Grid selection
            SQL = "SELECT " & GridCtrl1.TextMatrix(0, GridCtrl1.ColSel) & " FROM "
            & CurrentTable & " WHERE " & GridCtrl1.TextMatrix(0, GridCtrl1.ColSel)
            & " = '" & GridCtrl1.TextMatrix(GridCtrl1.RowSel, GridCtrl1.ColSel) & "'"

            'Create Recordset Object
            Dim RS As ADOCE.Recordset
            Set RS = CreateObject("ADOCE.Recordset.3.0")

            'A keyset-based, forward and backward, read and write Recordset
            RS.Open SQL, CN, adOpenKeyset, adLockOptimistic, adCmdText

            'Get dynamic user input
            For i = 0 To RS.Fields.Count - 1

                'Set new field equal to user input
```

```
            RS(RS.Fields(i).Name) = InputBox(RS.Fields(i).Name, "Add")

    Next

    'Ask user if he or she wants the record added
    If MsgBox("Do you wish to update this record?", vbYesNoCancel) =
    vbYes Then
        RS.Update
    Else
        RS.CancelUpdate
        MsgBox "No new record updated."
    End If

    RS.Close

    'Query the database again to refresh the Grid
    'A keyset-based, forward and backward, read and write Recordset
    RS.Open CurrentTable, CN, adOpenKeyset, adLockOptimistic, adCmdTable

    'Remove existing data from Grid
    GridCtrl1.Redraw = False
    For i = 1 To GridCtrl1.Rows
        GridCtrl1.RemoveItem 0
    Next

    'Set the Grid columns equal to the field count
    GridCtrl1.Cols = RS.Fields.Count

    'Get the column names
    For i = 0 To RS.Fields.Count - 1
        ColumnNames = ColumnNames & RS.Fields(i).Name & vbTab
    Next

    'Add the column headers to the Grid
    GridCtrl1.AddItem ColumnNames

    'Loop through the Recordset
    While Not RS.EOF

        'Get the column values for this row
        For i = 0 To RS.Fields.Count - 1
            ColumnValues = ColumnValues & RS.Fields(i).Value & vbTab
        Next
```

```
                    'Add the column values to the row
                    GridCtrl1.AddItem ColumnValues

                    'Set ColumnValues to a zero-length string
                    'so it can be refilled with the next row
                    ColumnValues = ""

                    RS.MoveNext

            Wend

            GridCtrl1.Redraw = True

            RS.Close

            Set RS = Nothing

        End If

    End If

End Sub
```

Sorting Data

Data that's viewed in the Grid is typically sorted based on the table's PrimaryKey index. When you want to sort your data based on a column other than the PrimaryKey, all you have to do is click the desired column header and select the Sort Selected Column menu item. The first thing you do in the code is build a new query to return everything from the current table ordered by the selected column header. From there on it's the same ViewData code that's used to fill the Grid, except this time, it's sorted to your liking. Create a Sub called "Sort-Data()" and add the following code:

```
Private Sub SortData()

    On Error Resume Next

    'Declare variables
    Dim i As Integer
    Dim ColumnNames As String
    Dim ColumnValues As String
```

```
Dim SQL As String

'Ensure that the following code is executed
'only if the user clicks a valid nonheader row.
If GridCtrl1.RowSel = 0 Then

    'Create Recordset Object
    Dim RS As ADOCE.Recordset
    Set RS = CreateObject("ADOCE.Recordset.3.0")

    SQL = "SELECT * FROM " & CurrentTable & " ORDER BY " &
                GridCtrl1.TextMatrix(GridCtrl1.RowSel, GridCtrl1.ColSel)

    'Return the data found in the cell at the intersection
    'of the selected row and column 0 to get the ContactID
    RS.Open SQL, CN, adOpenKeyset, adLockOptimistic, adCmdText

    'Remove existing data from Grid
    GridCtrl1.Redraw = False
    For i = 1 To GridCtrl1.Rows
        GridCtrl1.RemoveItem 0
    Next

    'Set the Grid columns equal to the field count
    GridCtrl1.Cols = RS.Fields.Count

    'Get the column names
    For i = 0 To RS.Fields.Count - 1
        GridCtrl1.ColWidth(i) = 1300
        ColumnNames = ColumnNames & RS.Fields(i).Name & vbTab
    Next

    'Add the column headers to the Grid
    GridCtrl1.AddItem ColumnNames

    'Loop through the Recordset
    While Not RS.EOF

        'Get the column values for this row
        For i = 0 To RS.Fields.Count - 1
            ColumnValues = ColumnValues & RS.Fields(i).Value & vbTab
        Next

        'Add the column values to the row
```

```
        GridCtrl1.AddItem ColumnValues

        'Set ColumnValues to a zero-length string
        'so it can be refilled with the next row
        ColumnValues = ""

        RS.MoveNext
    Wend

    GridCtrl1.Redraw = True

    'Close the Recordset
    RS.Close

    cmdDataView.Enabled = False
    cmdMetaDataView.Enabled = False
    cmdExecuteSQL.Enabled = True

    DataMenu.Items(1).Enabled = True      'Add Data
    DataMenu.Items(2).Enabled = True      'Update Selected Data
    DataMenu.Items(3).Enabled = True      'Delete Selected Data
    DataMenu.Items(4).Enabled = True      'Sort Selected Column

    TableMenu.Items(1).Enabled = False     'Add Table
    TableMenu.Items(2).Enabled = False     'Delete Selected Table
    TableMenu.Items(3).Enabled = False     'Rename Selected Table

    FieldMenu.Items(1).Enabled = False     'Add Field
    FieldMenu.Items(2).Enabled = False     'Delete Selected Field
    FieldMenu.Items(3).Enabled = False     'Rename Field
    FieldMenu.Items(4).Enabled = False     'Move Selected Field Up
    FieldMenu.Items(5).Enabled = False     'Move Selected Field Down
    FieldMenu.Items(7).Enabled = False     'Add Index
    FieldMenu.Items(8).Enabled = False     'Delete Selected Index

    Set RS = Nothing

  End If

End Sub
```

Querying Data

You've probably noticed the SQL Command Window sitting at the top of your form with its Execute SQL button always enabled as long as a database is open. What you have here is a TextBox with its Multiline property set to True so you can enter and execute free-form SQL statements whenever you like. The code to make this work is simple in that it just opens a Recordset based on the query entered in the TextBox. The results of the query are displayed in the Grid using code similar to the ViewData Sub. Create a Sub called "ViewSQL()" and add the following code:

```
Private Sub ViewSQL()

    On Error Resume Next

    'Declare variables
    Dim i As Integer
    Dim ColumnNames As String
    Dim ColumnValues As String

    If Trim(txtSQL.Text) <> "" Then

        'Create Recordset Object
        Dim RS As ADOCE.Recordset
        Set RS = CreateObject("ADOCE.Recordset.3.0")

        'Return the data found in the cell at the intersection
        'of the selected row and column 0 to get the ContactID
        RS.Open Trim(txtSQL.Text), CN, adOpenKeyset, adLockOptimistic, adCmdText

        'Remove existing data from Grid
        GridCtrl1.Redraw = False
        For i = 1 To GridCtrl1.Rows
            GridCtrl1.RemoveItem 0
        Next

        'Set the Grid columns equal to the field count
        GridCtrl1.Cols = RS.Fields.Count

        'Get the column names
        For i = 0 To RS.Fields.Count - 1
            GridCtrl1.ColWidth(i) = 1300
            ColumnNames = ColumnNames & RS.Fields(i).Name & vbTab
```

```
            Next

            'Add the column headers to the Grid
            GridCtrl1.AddItem ColumnNames

            'Loop through the Recordset
            While Not RS.EOF

                'Get the column values for this row
                For i = 0 To RS.Fields.Count - 1
                    ColumnValues = ColumnValues & RS.Fields(i).Value & vbTab
                Next

                'Add the column values to the row
                GridCtrl1.AddItem ColumnValues

                'Set ColumnValues to a zero-length string
                'so it can be refilled with the next row
                ColumnValues = ""

                RS.MoveNext
            Wend

            GridCtrl1.Redraw = True

            'Close the Recordset
            RS.Close

            cmdDataView.Enabled = False
            cmdMetaDataView.Enabled = False
            cmdExecuteSQL.Enabled = True

            DataMenu.Items(1).Enabled = True      'Add Data
            DataMenu.Items(2).Enabled = True      'Update Selected Data
            DataMenu.Items(3).Enabled = True      'Delete Selected Data
            DataMenu.Items(4).Enabled = True      'Sort Selected Column

            TableMenu.Items(1).Enabled = False     'Add Table
            TableMenu.Items(2).Enabled = False     'Delete Selected Table
            TableMenu.Items(3).Enabled = False     'Rename Selected Table

            FieldMenu.Items(1).Enabled = False     'Add Field
            FieldMenu.Items(2).Enabled = False     'Delete Selected Field
            FieldMenu.Items(3).Enabled = False     'Rename Field
```

```
                     FieldMenu.Items(4).Enabled = False    'Move Selected Field Up
                     FieldMenu.Items(5).Enabled = False    'Move Selected Field Down
                     FieldMenu.Items(7).Enabled = False    'Add Index
                     FieldMenu.Items(8).Enabled = False    'Delete Selected Index

                     Set RS = Nothing

             End If

     End Sub
```

Deleting Data

Whenever you're interested in deleting data, all you have to do is click anywhere in the row that you want to delete in the Grid and then select the Delete Selected Data menu item. You first build a query that returns only the row of data that you selected in the Grid. It's then a simple matter of calling the Delete method of the Recordset object to remove the row in question from the table. The remainder of the code is similar to the code found in the ViewData Sub. Create a Sub called "DeleteSelectedData()" and add the following code:

```
Private Sub DeleteSelectedData()

    On Error Resume Next

    'Declare variables
    Dim i As Integer
    Dim ColumnNames As String
    Dim ColumnValues As String
    Dim SQL As String

    If GridCtrl1.RowSel > 0 Then

        If GridCtrl1.TextMatrix(GridCtrl1.RowSel, GridCtrl1.ColSel) <> "" Then

            SQL = "SELECT * FROM " & CurrentTable & " WHERE " &
            GridCtrl1.TextMatrix(0, GridCtrl1.ColSel) & " = '" &
            GridCtrl1.TextMatrix(GridCtrl1.RowSel, GridCtrl1.ColSel) & "'"
```

```
'Create Recordset Object
Dim RS As ADOCE.Recordset
Set RS = CreateObject("ADOCE.Recordset.3.0")

'A keyset-based, forward and backward, read and write Recordset
RS.Open SQL, CN, adOpenKeyset, adLockOptimistic, adCmdText

'Ask user if he or she wants the record added
If MsgBox("Do you wish to delete this record?", vbYesNoCancel) =
vbYes Then
    RS.Delete
Else
    'RS.CancelUpdate
    MsgBox "The record is unchanged."
End If

RS.Close

'Query the database again to refresh the Grid
'A keyset-based, forward and backward, read and write Recordset
RS.Open CurrentTable, CN, adOpenKeyset, adLockOptimistic, adCmdTable

'Remove existing data from Grid
GridCtrl1.Redraw = False
For i = 1 To GridCtrl1.Rows
    GridCtrl1.RemoveItem 0
Next

'Set the Grid columns equal to the field count
GridCtrl1.Cols = RS.Fields.Count

'Get the column names
For i = 0 To RS.Fields.Count - 1
    ColumnNames = ColumnNames & RS.Fields(i).Name & vbTab
Next

'Add the column headers to the Grid
GridCtrl1.AddItem ColumnNames

'Loop through the Recordset
While Not RS.EOF
```

```
                        'Get the column values for this row
                        For i = 0 To RS.Fields.Count - 1
                            ColumnValues = ColumnValues & RS.Fields(i).Value & vbTab
                        Next

                        'Add the column values to the row
                        GridCtrl1.AddItem ColumnValues

                        'Set ColumnValues to a zero-length string
                        'so it can be refilled with the next row
                        ColumnValues = ""

                        RS.MoveNext

                    Wend

                    GridCtrl1.Redraw = True

                    RS.Close

                    Set RS = Nothing

                End If

            End If

        End Sub
```

Loose Ends

Even though you've now created all the Subs necessary to make the application function, there are several click events that need to call these Subs:

- Form_OKClick—Shutdown

- cmdDataView_Click—ViewData

- cmdExecuteSQL_Click—ViewSQL

- cmdMetaDataView—ViewMetaData

- cmdTableView—ViewTables

That should wrap everything up for all the CommandButtons in the Pocket Access application.

You Made It!

Congratulations on assembling a full-featured Pocket Access database manager! I think you'll find it to be a handy item to have residing on your Pocket PC. You can't always rely on having Microsoft Access around to build and manage databases for you, particularly when you're on the road and away from your desktop computer. More important, you now possess the skills to build any kind of database application imaginable for the Pocket PC, and it wasn't that hard either. At the beginning of the book you learned how to implement both the DDL and DML using ADOCE and eMbedded Visual Basic. You then learned all the nuances of the ADOCE Connection and Recordset objects. Finally, you learned how to communicate with both desktop and enterprise databases from your Pocket PC using ActiveSync. Now you've pulled all those skills together to build a graphical database management tool for your Pocket Access databases.

Let's talk about where you go from here. The only thing that makes an operating system or a particular hardware platform successful is having a critical mass of desirable applications available for that platform. In the '80s and '90s, Microsoft found its DOS and Windows operating systems constantly fighting the market-share war against worthy opponents like OS/2, CPM, and Macintosh. The reason Microsoft won out over those other players wasn't necessarily because they had a better product, but because they did whatever it took to get software application developers like you to write applications for their platform.

Now there's a handheld computing war going on between the Palm and the Pocket PC. The Pocket PC's ability to erase the Palm's market-share lead rests on the shoulders of innovative hardware manufacturers like Compaq, with its stylish iPAQ, and software developers like you who need to build up that critical mass of applications. Take what you've learned in this book and show your colleagues and the people you work for that viable enterprise application development is possible on the Pocket PC. Once CIOs, CTOs, IT directors, and IT managers realize that the Pocket PC isn't just a PDA used for maintaining addresses and appointments, projects to build vertical applications will be authorized andsoftware developers who are on the first wave of this phenomenon will lead those projects. Many of the tools you need are right in this book. Other enabling technologies, such as Message Queuing, SOAP, and .NET, are either here now or just around the corner. Help to fuel this new computing revolution by thinking back to all the desktop, client/server, and Web applications you've built over the last ten years and envision how those same applications could run on the Pocket PC to empower today's mobile workforce.

I sincerely hope you've found this book to be helpful in your quest to be a more proficient Pocket PC developer. My own career as a programmer wouldn't have ever gotten off the ground if it weren't for relevant books with lots of examples. I've tried my best to be concise and let the examples do the talking because there's a big difference between explaining something to someone and showing that person how it's done. Good luck with your Pocket PC programming.

Index

books for professionals by professionals™

About Apress

Apress, located in Berkeley, CA, is an innovative publishing company devoted to meeting the needs of existing and potential programming professionals. Simply put, the "A" in Apress stands for the "Author's Press™." Apress' unique author-centric approach to publishing grew from conversations between Dan Appleman and Gary Cornell, authors of best-selling, highly regarded computer books. In 1998, they set out to create a publishing company that emphasized quality above all else, a company with books that would be considered the best in their market. Dan and Gary's vision has resulted in over 30 widely acclaimed titles by some of the industry's leading software professionals.

Do You Have What It Takes to Write for Apress?

Apress is rapidly expanding its publishing program. If you can write and refuse to compromise on the quality of your work, if you believe in doing more then rehashing existing documentation, and if you're looking for opportunities and rewards that go far beyond those offered by traditional publishing houses, we want to hear from you!

Consider these innovations that we offer all of our authors:

- **Top royalties with *no* hidden switch statements**
  Authors typically only receive half of their normal royalty rate on foreign sales. In contrast, Apress' royalty rate remains the same for both foreign and domestic sales.

- **A mechanism for authors to obtain equity in Apress**
  Unlike the software industry, where stock options are essential to motivate and retain software professionals, the publishing industry has adhered to an outdated compensation model based on royalties alone. In the spirit of most software companies, Apress reserves a significant portion of its equity for authors.

- **Serious treatment of the technical review process**
  Each Apress book has a technical reviewing team whose remuneration depends in part on the success of the book since they too receive royalties.

Moreover, through a partnership with Springer-Verlag, one of the world's major publishing houses, Apress has significant venture capital behind it. Thus, we have the resources to produce the highest quality books *and* market them aggressively.

If you fit the model of the Apress author who can write a book that gives the "professional what he or she needs to know™," then please contact one of our Editorial Directors, Gary Cornell (gary_cornell@apress.com), Dan Appleman (dan_appleman@apress.com), Karen Watterson (karen_watterson@apress.com) or Jason Gilmore (jason_gilmore@apress.com) for more information.

Apress Titles

ISBN	LIST PRICE	AUTHOR	TITLE
1-893115-01-1	$39.95	Appleman	Appleman's Win32 API Puzzle Book and Tutorial for Visual Basic Programmers
1-893115-23-2	$29.95	Appleman	How Computer Programming Works
1-893115-97-6	$39.95	Appleman	Moving to VB.NET: Strategies, Concepts and Code
1-893115-09-7	$29.95	Baum	Dave Baum's Definitive Guide to LEGO MINDSTORMS
1-893115-84-4	$29.95	Baum, Gasperi, Hempel, and Villa	Extreme MINDSTORMS
1-893115-82-8	$59.95	Ben-Gan/Moreau	Advanced Transact-SQL for SQL Server 2000
1-893115-85-2	$34.95	Gilmore	A Programmer's Introduction to PHP 4.0
1-893115-17-8	$59.95	Gross	A Programmer's Introduction to Windows DNA
1-893115-62-3	$39.95	Gunnerson	A Programmer's Introduction to C#, Second Edition
1-893115-10-0	$34.95	Holub	Taming Java Threads
1-893115-04-6	$34.95	Hyman/Vaddadi	Mike and Phani's Essential C++ Techniques
1-893115-50-X	$34.95	Knudsen	Wireless Java: Developing with Java 2, Micro Edition
1-893115-79-8	$49.95	Kofler	Definitive Guide to Excel VBA
1-893115-56-9	$39.95	Kofler/Kramer	MySQL
1-893115-75-5	$44.95	Kurniawan	Internet Programming with VB
1-893115-19-4	$49.95	Macdonald	Serious ADO: Universal Data Access with Visual Basic
1-893115-06-2	$39.95	Marquis/Smith	A Visual Basic 6.0 Programmer's Toolkit
1-893115-22-4	$27.95	McCarter	David McCarter's VB Tips and Techniques
1-893115-76-3	$49.95	Morrison	C++ For VB Programmers
1-893115-80-1	$39.95	Newmarch	A Programmer's Guide to Jini Technology

ISBN	LIST PRICE	AUTHOR	TITLE
1-893115-81-X	$39.95	Pike	SQL Server: Common Problems, Tested Solutions
1-893115-20-8	$34.95	Rischpater	Wireless Web Development
1-893115-93-3	$34.95	Rischpater	Wireless Web Development with PHP and WAP
1-893115-24-0	$49.95	Sinclair	From Access to SQL Server
1-893115-94-1	$29.95	Spolsky	User Interface Design for Programmers
1-893115-53-4	$39.95	Sweeney	Visual Basic for Testers
1-893115-65-8	$39.95	Tiffany	Pocket PC Database Development with eMbedded Visual Basic
1-893115-59-3	$59.95	Troelsen	C# and the .NET Platform
1-893115-54-2	$49.95	Trueblood/Lovett	Data Mining and Statistical Analysis Using SQL
1-893115-16-X	$49.95	Vaughn	ADO Examples and Best Practices
1-893115-83-6	$44.95	Wells	Code Centric: T-SQL Programming with Stored Procedures and Triggers
1-893115-95-X	$49.95	Welschenbach	Cryptography in C and C++
1-893115-05-4	$39.95	Williamson	Writing Cross-Browser Dynamic HTML
1-893115-78-X	$49.95	Zukowski	Definitive Guide to Swing for Java 2, Second Edition
1-893115-92-5	$49.95	Zukowski	Java Collections

Available at bookstores nationwide or from Springer Verlag New York, Inc. at 1-800-777-4643; fax 1-212-533-3503. Contact us for more information at sales@apress.com.

Apress Titles Publishing SOON!

ISBN	AUTHOR	TITLE
1-893115-99-2	Cornell/Morrison	Programming VB.NET: A Guide for Experienced Programmers
1-893115-72-0	Curtin	Trust: Online Security for Developers
1-893115-55-0	Frenz	Visual Basic for Scientists
1-893115-96-8	Jorelid	J2EE FrontEnd Technologies: A Programmer's Guide to Servlets, JavaServer Pages, and Enterprise
1-893115-87-9	Kurata	Doing Web Development: Client-Side Techniques
1-893115-58-5	Oellerman	Fundamental Web Services with XML
1-893115-89-5	Shemitz	Kylix: The Professional Developer's Guide and Reference
1-893115-29-1	Thomsen	Database Programming with VB.NET

Available at bookstores nationwide or from Springer Verlag New York, Inc. at 1-800-777-4643; fax 1-212-533-3503. Contact us for more information at sales@apress.com.

Everything's Coming-Up
WIRELESS

Wireless Web Development

by Ray Rischpater

ISBN: 1-893115-20-8
$34.95

Wireless JAVA

by Jonathan Knudsen

ISBN: 1-893115-50-X
$34.95

The wireless Web is quickly becoming an integral part of any successful organization's informational infrastructure. *Wireless Web Development* and *Wireless Java* show readers how to make the most of wireless technologies to create truly dynamic, scalable wireless applications.

Books for Professionals by Professionals™